SO-ADZ-380

PLACE IN RETURN BOX to remove this checkout from your record.
TO AVOID FINES return on or before date due.

DATE DUE	DATE DUE	DATE DUE
FEB 0 7 1994	FEB 0 6 1996	
2 3 9		
FEB 0 3 1994	APR 1 4 1996	
JUN 1 3 1996	JUN	
4 9 1		

01

THE FUTURE OF TELEVISION

A Global Overview of Programming, Advertising, Technology, and Growth

Marc Doyle

The National Association of
Television Program Executives

NTC Business Books
a division of *NTC Publishing Group* • Lincolnwood, Illinois USA

Library of Congress Cataloging-in-Publication Data

Doyle, Marc.
    The future of television : a global overview of programming,
advertising, technology, and growth / Marc Doyle.
        p.   cm.

    1. Television broadcasting.   I. Title.
    HE8700.4.D69   1992
384.55--dc20   91-44640
                                                            CIP

Published by NTC Business Books, a division of NTC Publishing Group
4255 West Touhy Avenue
Lincolnwood (Chicago), Illinois 60646-1975, U.S.A.
© 1992 by NTC Business Books. All rights reserved.
No part of this book may be reproduced, stored in a retrieval system,
or transmitted in any form or by any means,
electronic, mechanical, photocopying, recording or otherwise,
without the prior permission of NTC Publishing Group.
Manufactured in the United States of America.

2 3 4 5 6 7 8 9 0 VP 9 8 7 6 5 4 3 2 1

6890179

INTERNATIONAL

The National Association of Television Program Executives

NATPE International is a nonprofit organization dedicated to furthering excellence in television programming. It is comprised of key decision makers in the television industry, with a membership of over 2,000 executives, representatives, group broadcast companies, networks, cable organizations, syndicators, and program distributors.

In 1987, one of the objectives of a new Five Year Plan for NATPE International was the commitment to publish a book on the "future of television programming around the world." That objective has been met. This book, underwritten by NATPE International and the NATPE Educational Foundation, is the result of nearly two years of work by Marc Doyle.

Interviews were conducted in many parts of the world. It is filled with fact and projection. It is a Who's Who of the television program and production industry. I am sure you will find these pages interesting, informative, and thought-provoking.

Phil Corvo
President
NATPE International

Foreword

What come most readily to mind when I look back on nearly
forty years of covering television (man and boy, I like to say)
are the historic turning points. There were a scant few of them,
perhaps only four in that four-decade span, but I won't quarrel
with any suggestion of a fifth or sixth. These were developments
whose mighty waves of change rocked the industry off its charted
course. When they occurred, these turning points, you knew the
television business was never going to be the same.

These were times when everyone in the industry became suddenly obsessed with the future—not the near future of the next
business quarter, but the future beyond that, the future that
people working in the industry would have to adapt to and live
in for the rest of time (or at least until something else unforeseen

came along to make the waves again). Each turning point was a reminder that history does not move in a straight line and that the future is not the present projected forward.

The first of the turning points was Ampex's introduction of videotape at the 1956 National Association of Broadcasters convention. What a bombshell it was; everyone there thought they witnessed a miracle. The excitement was palpable, and it was happy excitement. Television became a new medium then, and the industry took a marked turn.

It took another turn in 1970 when the Federal Communications Commission acted to reconstruct the marketplace by legislating the networks out of program ownership, cable ownership, and domestic syndication with the Financial Interest and Syndication Rule. In that same breath, the FCC reduced the networks' claim on prime time to three hours a night with the Prime-Time Access Rule. Bang—the old system of total domination by the networks was dead. I had expected that year's National Association of Television Program Executives convention to ring with jubilation, but instead there was angst and gloom. Clearly this was a change that took some getting used to. That didn't take too long, however—just until the first beautiful profit statements. Today the mere suggestion of repealing prime access could start a brawl.

Everything proceeded along a smooth, failure-proof course until the next momentous episode: the discovery in 1975 that satellites made possible instant national networks on cable. HBO was the one to prove it, and its success propelled the spread of cable in the '80s, fragmenting the audience over 30 or more channels and turning the old television economy on its head. The National Cable Television Association conventions of the early '80s were charged with excitement. Everyone who smelled money was there. New cable networks were epidemic. This was a revolution in the making, though it took a few years to make itself felt. Today we realize all too well that what we witnessed then was the end of television as we had known it.

Fourth was the deregulation of broadcasting and cable in the mid-'80s, occurring coincidentally (or maybe not so coincidentally) with wholesale changes of ownership in the industry. Not only the networks but virtually every major broadcast group was sold or broken up. The changing of the guard in the new free-market climate meant a change in the whole value system of television, turning it from an aspiring profession to a business that is strictly business all down the line, and heavily leveraged to boot.

I recount these high points of history for a reason: to lend perspective to the new turning point, the fifth one, that has come on more quietly than the others, without (so far) a severe jolt. Still there are the waves, and they are ever so subtly moving the American television industry onto yet another new course, though many in the business are still unaware it is happening.

This new wave of change is the internationalizing of television. What this means ultimately, I believe, is an end to American insularity. Every major country in the world has access to the same technologies as we, most European countries have adopted commercial and pay-television for the first time, and nearly all are following the American lead in deregulating. For the first time in history, operators in such countries as Germany, France, and Spain are in the same business as broadcasters in the U.S. (Italy got there earlier, and the U.K. too, but only about half way.)

This has the sound of new markets opening for American programming exports, and many television practitioners view it in just that light—the expansion of an ancillary market to gorgeous proportions. Indeed, that's what it has been for the past five years: Profit City for a lot of program suppliers. Some American distributors have been feasting on the foreign markets to the exclusion of domestic syndication. Every new channel that lights up in Europe, the Pacific Rim, and Latin America needs a ton of serviceable, inexpensive programming to start—and there's no better source than the U.S. suppliers.

But selling to these new systems is just Phase 1 in this extraordinary development. Already we've begun buying from foreign suppliers, which is Phase 2. At this, the cable networks have taken the lead, but CBS's latenight checkerboard is dominated by Canadian productions, and ABC's big surprise hit, America's Funniest Home Videos, is in fact a knockoff of a Japanese series.

The countries that never had commercial television before also never had a community of independent production companies. But today such companies are sprouting up everywhere and forming coproduction partnerships to afford expensive projects. And their mission by and large is the same as that of their American counterparts—to produce entertainment for the largest possible audience. Producing commercial entertainment is not rocket science after all, and while American companies have without question been best at it these many years they've had a long head start. Not forgotten is that the United States was also once the world leader in electronics manufacture and for decades—we thought forever—produced the automobiles of choice for its own citizenry. Other countries do catch up and can seize a market from the complacent.

The TV developments abroad coincide with the softening of the U.S. television market's vaunted self-sufficiency. Increasingly, with the continuing dispersal of the audience over varied channels, it gets harder to produce for the domestic market alone. Meanwhile, the major networks continue to search for solutions to rising program costs in the face of shrinking audiences.

Things are taking a turn. The United States, which long has exported the most television while importing the least (outside the People's Republic of China), is steadily becoming part of a world television community. Even as foreign conglomerates have been acquiring Hollywood studios, American operators—notably CapCities/ABC—have been buying into European production companies or forming tight partnerships, recognizing that together the 12 countries of the Common Market are one-third larger than the United States. If and when the American networks are ever freed from the financial interest rule, they will surely take an interest in foreign markets and will select programs not only for domestic audiences but for those abroad as well.

The '90s are bound to be more a turnstile than a mere historic turning point, because the expansion of television's canvas to global proportions is only part of what is bringing on change. Technology refuses to stop and take a breath. Just when fiber-optics have become affordable for cable installations, compression technology is being perfected for satellites and cable to multiply each existing transponder and channel by at least five. Well before the year 2000 most American households, and doubtless some abroad, will have the ability to receive 150 or more channels of television. Some form of high-definition or advanced TV will be operational, and we will surely in this decade be well acquainted with interactive television. This is not futuristic talk; all these developments are present tense.

It's all so mind-boggling. Where does one go to get a handle on it? What's needed is a guide to the future, or more aptly a guide to the developments that will be shaping the future, however it may all turn out.

One day recently it arrived on my desk; Marc Doyle's perceptive and well-researched manuscript. Wow, how neatly done and perfectly timed. What I like especially about it is its straightforwardness and sobriety. It does not pretend to futurism (something, I'm aware, I myself may be accused of) but simply lays out what has to be considered in a time when we are all (or should be) future-minded again.

I'm told the ancient Chinese had no actual word for the future but in their writing represented it by joining two calligraphic characters. One was the symbol for opportunity, the other for peril. This is still as good a definition for it as I have ever heard.

Les Brown
New York City
October 1991

Les Brown is currently writing his seventh book. He founded Channels magazine and Television Business International. Formerly, Mr. Brown was television correspondent for The New York Times and television editor for Variety.

Contents

CHAPTER ONE

The Stage Is Set

As the television industry throughout the world approaches the next millennium, the historic year 2000 A.D., the stage is set for a decade of dramatic and revolutionary change. By all accounts the 1990s promise a rate and speed of change that will make previous decades uneventful by comparison. Without question, managing change smartly and profitably is the greatest challenge facing the television industry today.

Before venturing into the television world of tomorrow, we will look back briefly. With the benefit of hindsight, we can understand the factors that have led us to where we are today. That understanding of the past will then become our point of reference as we peer out into the mysterious realm of the future of television.

1

The End of the Mass Market

The world of television was revolutionized by several distinct trends during the 1980s. The most obvious trend was the breaking up of the traditional mass television audience into fragmented segments of smaller audiences. Dozens of satellite-delivered cable program services, hundreds of new independent local TV stations, and millions of video cassette recorders provided a staggering increase in program choices for television viewers.

> Not much more than a decade ago, we had essentially 2½ national networks, with ABC as the weak sister. Today, we have a solid three networks—ABC, CBS and NBC—and a fourth, Fox Broadcasting, closing fast. They are competing with a cable television industry that passes some 90 percent of American homes and provides 30 or more channels to six out of every seven who subscribe. The cable networks also reach several million additional people through home satellite receivers. The number of independent TV outlets has more than quintupled, going from 64 to 330. Program producers, moreover, are also not as dependent on the national networks as once was the case. Producers have gained a new $4 billion a year in revenues from the video cassette market, for example. They have also attained a world programming sales market which yields well over one billion dollars annually.
>
> Al Sikes, Chairman
> Federal Communications
> Commission

The revolution in viewer choice has not been limited to the United States. In Europe, country after country has deregulated its broadcast system and opened the doors to commercialization of television. For European viewers the increase in program choices is dramatic. Experts estimate that the number of hours of television programming delivered to European viewers will grow from 220,000 in 1987 to 500,000 in 1995.

Stewart Butterfield, European Media Director of McCann Erickson, estimates that the number of commercial network channels in Western Europe will increase from 26 in 1980 to 90 in the mid-1990s.

In a nutshell, the single most important change in Europe can be summed up in the word "deregulation," the freeing up of the airwaves by the government or by states that have traditionally controlled broadcasting, and the coming of private enterprise into the system, particularly in mainland Europe where you have had a large number of private stations start operating and they have had an extraordinary effect upon the way the state stations operate.

Brian Jacobs
Vice Chairman and Executive
Media Director
Leo Burnett Advertising

The fragmenting of the traditional mass television market has impacted every dimension of the television industry. Advertisers, the commercial life blood of the business, now have many more ways to reach their customers. But this increased opportunity for advertisers has not come without a price.

An important trend is the unevenness of the research and other data to support all of these media vehicles. We have more numbers than we probably would ever want to look at. And, a lot of them are apples and oranges. There really are not any nice analytical packages to put them all together, so we find ourselves dealing with just gobs of numbers.

Jayne Spittler
Vice President of Media
Research
Leo Burnett Advertising

Despite the fact that 60 percent of the households in the United States subscribe to cable TV, and most of those households receive somewhere between 30 and 60 channels, for many Americans that's just not enough. Every day millions of people in the United States visit their neighborhood video store to rent videotapes—and they don't have far to go. It sometimes seems that every intersection in America has at least one video store. Home video is a major contributor to the dissemination of the traditional television audience. A 1990 study by Alexander and Associates reports that more than 35 million TV households are tuned to their VCRs during prime time every week. According to the study, on Friday and Saturday nights 9 million homes, representing 10 percent of all the households in America, are watching videos. The study's consultant, Andrew Marrus, in analyzing his data, describes video consumers as "choosing to pay cash for their entertainment decision instead of taking a passive role and watching free network television."[1]

In the early stages of the 1990s one of the prime realities for the television industry is that the explosion of program distribution sources has radically and forever changed the nature of the business. Gone are the days of a neatly carved mass marketplace. Today's segmented television marketplace reflects the enormously competitive battle to attract customers who have a dizzying number of choices—and there seems to be no end in sight.

> I see continued fractionalization . . . you're going to see the further expansion of the number of choices that are available to people. That's just clear. That's not a trend. That's the only environment in which we will all function.
>
> Barry Diller
> Chairman & CEO, Fox Inc.

Financial Restructuring

The second major new reality confronting the television industry involves financial restructuring. During the 1980s capital investment poured into the entertainment and media industry and spilled over into every operating crevice in the business. In 1986 alone, $4 billion of investment capital was raised for media companies in the United States.

This essentially unregulated torrent of money flowing into the industry fueled some of the most spectacular events in the history of the television business. During the '80s all three major national networks changed ownership. Local television stations were bought and sold like pork bellies. It seemed that nearly every issue of the weekly trade publications heralded yet another historic financial deal. The unbounded financial optimism of the '80s made the guessing game of "who would takeover whom next" one of the favored pastimes of industry insiders, from studio moguls in Hollywood to local station production crews in Tampa.

As the new decade begins, however, the euphoria of the '80s has given way to sober reflection.

> In that particular rising tide environment, investors, lenders, and buyers of media assets were clearly overlooking a series of ominous microtrends. What the financial markets chose to ignore, even though the signs were there, is that there was no longer a viable assumption that there would be uninterrupted growth in advertiser spending. So, add this dramatic slowing in advertising expenditures to the threat of cable reregulation, and, in a very short period of time, it stunned everybody. Yesterday's optimists became today's doubters.
> Entrepreneurs and media barons who automatically assumed that their visions would become financial reality are now forced to retool their balance sheets and stop dreaming.
>
> Fred Segal
> Salomon Brothers

The new economic realities of the '90s, fueled by the go-go years of the '80s, have affected every dimension of the television industry. As companies institute wave after wave of cost control measures, employees are being told to do more with less. In order to survive and prosper, companies routinely consider new approaches to business that would have been unthinkable a few short years ago.

> The driving forces of the industry today basically start with a consolidation that's been going on for the last couple of years. That consolidation is brought about by a number of factors, not the least of which is the drying up of the capital markets. So, entrepreneurial companies which were the focus of the industry in the decade of the '80s find it very difficult

to exist and compete today because they don't have the
capital to really build and expand their operations. That's an
important factor. But, that really serves as a catalyst to
trigger what has now become a major consolidation of the
industry. I'd say for the next decade the competitive factors
are going to principally be scale. The smaller companies are
finding it very hard to compete because the price of
everything has gone up. The risks essentially have become
the game for big companies.

> Michael Garin
> Senior Managing Director
> Furman, Selz

Investment bankers and financial entrepreneurs have plenty
of company in the nervous economic reality of the early '90s.
Rich Colbert, head of sales for I.T.C. Entertainment Group,
describes the marketplace for new television programming as
"hostile." As the advertising slowdown forces television stations
to tighten their belts, analysis of the risk–reward ratio in program purchasing has become what some executives call "career
decisions." The net result is a reduction in the willingness of
television stations to assume risks for new programs. Stations
are reluctant to change even marginal programming, fearing
the new replacement programming might not perform as well.
Short-term contracts and tiering of program schedules are the
norm. License fees, for anything other than proven winners, are
constantly pushed lower and lower.

One of the major forces affecting the production/distribution
business over the past few years is the bursting of the
financial bubble that had fueled the syndication market in
the middle '80s.

> Frank Mancuso
> Former Chairman and CEO
> Paramount Pictures

The launch of the Fox network, the increase in local news programming, and the solid entrenchment of the highest-rated

shows, have dramatically altered the environment for beginning new programs. The big Hollywood production/distribution companies are struggling to deal with their new economic realities.

> There are two things that are really impacting on production and distribution and they are intertwined. One is the production side—the gigantic increases in the cost to get these shows made. You're now looking at half-hour network shows that are running at between $500,000 and $750,000, and hours that are at least $1.2 million or $1.3 million. Set against that, you have three networks that are newly owned and are very bottom-line oriented companies who are trying to push costs down as much as possible. Set that against the background of a lot of television stations being squeezed and not having a lot of money to buy expensive off-network shows. Then Fox, while it becomes another buyer on the network side, takes up a giant amount of programming opportunities on the station side. In other words, when they program prime time, right away the ability to sell movies and off-network movies to independents is virtually taken away except for the occasional package. So, you have four networks feeding product into a reduced demand area which is driving down the syndication prices. Those things brought to bear on each other are making life very difficult on the production side.
>
> Rich Frank, President
> Walt Disney Studios

In the boardrooms of corporate media companies, in strategy sessions at local TV stations, and in program development meetings in Hollywood, the television industry is hammering out its agenda to manage the risky economic environment of the new decade.

Globalization

The third major new reality confronting the television business at the dawn of the '90s is the globalization of the industry. The fractionalizing of the mass audience during the '80s was greeted with mixed reviews. It was a problem if you were a traditional over-the-air network or affiliate. It was a great opportunity if you were a satellite cable program service. The financial restructuring of the '80s was also a double-edged sword. Many stockholders of restructured companies reaped enormous profits when the value of their stock was driven to record heights. Some companies emerged from the merger, acquisition, and takeover mania stronger than ever before. But other companies stumbled and tripped into the '90s, burdened down under the weight of paralyzing debt.

However, globalization of television has been generally a positive development over the past ten years. It confirms America's position as the television capital of the world. Globalization, with its cross country mergers, its international coproductions, and its burgeoning program sales opportunities, is partly a result of deregulating the non-U.S. television markets. But, it was also fueled by corporate America's insatiable appetite for growth.

> The stock market, which had supported rapid growth for almost all sectors of the entertainment business, has become skeptical of anybody who talks about synergies, talks about turnarounds. All they care about now, once again, as they used to before the decade of the '80s, is what are near-term earnings going to be like. Now, with that gloomy assessment, what does it mean? It means that both large and small companies in the United States are forced to look beyond the U.S. border in order to find their sustenance. The larger companies, to the extent they are free from regulatory constraints, are going to have to look outside the United States where they are constrained significantly. Both Capital Cities and NBC have already made small, embryonic but nonetheless, I think, significant entries into foreign media markets. The smaller companies are going to have to look outside the United States for capital. Companies like Carolco, MTM, and Reeves have already done that. More are on the way. Large companies as well will have to go outside the United States for sources of [risk] capital.
>
> Fred Segal
> Salomon Brothers

The popularity of American programming throughout the world is so generally recognized that it even has become a trendy topic in the business press as well as television magazine programs. The bestseller book *Megatrends 2000* reports that 75 percent of all internationally imported television programs come from the United States. We are alerted that Dallas is seen in nearly 100 countries, that Mickey Mouse and Donald Duck are dubbed into Mandarin and shown weekly in China, and that la roue de la fortune is the hottest gameshow on French television.

> Globalization is really driven by a couple of factors. Number one is the change in the United States which has made deficits greater and forced people to look at the international value of their products to make up for the deficit. Secondly, the changes that have gone on overseas, at the same time, which have enhanced those values; namely, the privatization of broadcasting and the same kinds of technological changes, cable, home video, and DBS, which have created new markets and competition for product which has bid up the prices. So, basically, I would say what this is about is about money first and creativity second.
>
> Michael Garin
> Senior Managing Director
> Furman, Selz

By the end of 1990, four of the seven major Hollywood studios, including their television divisions, were owned by non-U.S. companies. This dramatic development in the globalization of the entertainment industry occurred with shocking speed and was greeted with mixed reaction throughout the business world. In the wake of the Japanese takeovers, Columbia and MCA both gained access to new capital and emerged with stronger financial leverage for future expansion. Following Matsushitas's purchase of MCA Inc., Sidney Sheinberg, president of MCA, was quoted in *Electronic Media* as having no doubt that in today's world bigger is better. "The reality is we can't go back to the way things were. We're entering the twenty-first century, and we better be prepared to move into that future in some way that is compatible with the new requirements of the marketplace."

But the global mega-deals are not without their critics. Some question whether there really is a business strategy beyond the predictable talk of synergies between hardware and software. Others point out the potential political fallout if Americans begin to think that Hollywood's creativity is being controlled from Japan. Still others question whether Sony's and Matsushita's management can effectively run creatively driven companies that are so essentially different from consumer electronics manufacturing.

Cross-country corporate globalization is an unproven strategy, but international coproduction of television programming became a well-established and generally accepted strategy in the '80s. One of the major coproduction hurdles—the inability of non-U.S. productions to break into prime time on the major U.S. networks—appears to have been cleared by CBS and Granada Television. The U.K. commercial ITV station will coproduce, with CBS, a group of six made-for-television movies over the next three years.

These international program partnerships, born out of the need to reduce front-end production expenses, have developed into a normal and accepted business practice for producers and distributors in all the major media markets of the world. The makers, packagers, distributors, and users of television programs meet in what seems like an endless series of annual conferences to hammer out their coproduction deals. The development of small cassette videotapes, the emergence of global satellite delivery systems, and the availability of fax machines have turned the program selling business into a year-round activity in all territories of the globe. The face-to-face negotiating at NATPE, at Monte Carlo, at MIP and MIPCOM is the forum that facilitates coproduction agreements. International coproductions abound in the '90s.

- CapCities/ABC and ZDF, a leading German broadcaster, have a long-term coproduction agreement to create TV movies, series, documentaries, music programs, and variety shows for the international marketplace. The agreement also involves Tele-Munchen, a TV production and distribution company in Munich, in which ABC Video Enterprises owns a 49 percent interest.

- CBS Entertainment and the BBC have entered into an international agreement to develop four comedy scripts.

- Granada TV, in the United Kingdom, is coproducing eight TV movies for HBO.

- Central TV, also in the United Kingdom, is developing TV movies with Hollywood-based Ventura Entertainment and Australia's Grundy International.

- Two other ITV companies have acquired American companies to improve their coproduction leverage. TVS bought MTM and Thames acquired Reeves Entertainment.

- NBC and Yorkshire TV have formed Tango Productions to coproduce for the international marketplace.

- Central TV teamed up with Belbo Film Productions in the Netherlands to produce the movie Vincent and Theo.

- Silvio Burlusconi Communications (Italy), TF1 (France), and Leo Kirch's Beta Film (Germany) coproduced Phantom of the Opera starring Burt Lancaster and directed by Tony Richardson. In addition to a successful European performance, Phantom attracted 20% of people watching television to NBC in 1990.

- RAI 2 (Italy), Beta Group's Taurus Films (Germany), and Tribune Entertainment (United States) teamed up for the coproduction of Voyage of Terror: The Achille Lauro Affair, which successfully aired in media markets throughout the world.

The explosion in international coproduction activity began in the mid-'80s. It was ignited by companies looking beyond their own marketplaces for complementary opportunities to offset their own financial shortfalls. Hollywood needed a way to balance the impact of reduced network license fees and a softening of the syndication market. Networks and TV stations were looking for ways to recoup lost advertising revenues resulting from smaller, fragmented audiences. European broadcasters, facing stiff new competition resulting from deregulation, desperately needed to lower their development and production expenses.

Once the financial dealmakers filed their contracts and spreadsheets and went on to the next deal, the job of actually creating and executing the international coproductions fell to the creative people from the various companies involved. It was at this stage that a number of coproductions got into trouble. The old adage of a camel being a horse designed by a committee seems appropriate.

> We're probably doing more coproductions than anyone, but there are problems as well as advantages. It costs less but you have to have a production that is compromised to a degree. Productions that are compromised for the world markets don't do that well here in the United States. We're really looking forward to seeing our program on the life of Michelangelo that we did with RAI. The coproductions they have done have been very good over the years.
>
> Ted Turner, Chairman
> Turner Broadcasting System

International coproductions are a way of life in the new global world of television. But, the financially driven deals of the mid-'80s rapidly gave way to the creatively driven alliances of the late-'80s. As networks, producers, and distributors on both sides of the ocean gained more practical experience in the coproduction business, they were reminded that viewers watch programs, not "deals." To be successful a coproduction deal must not only reduce the financial risk of the partners, it must first and foremost appeal to the television viewers in the markets where it is shown. Creativity is back on the front burner in the coproduction arena in the 1990s.

> I believe that television will come out of what I consider its parochial past. We have to a large extent been within our own boundaries and our own shores. Political change and economic change are forcing closer alliances between people involved in the creative process. We call them coproductions, coventures, cofinancing; but I think increasingly it's going to

be the exchange of ideas among creative people that leads to the television programs of the future as opposed to them necessarily being financially led. I think they will be creatively led. The spark for that has no doubt been the introduction of more commercial systems into parts of the world other than the United States. In the United States you have had it for years. But the effect that cable and satellites and new competition has had inside the United Kingdom and inside Europe is very significant, and, I think, of major importance to the United States. There is a creative energy in the United Kingdom, in France, and in Germany that is being released now.

> David Plowright, Chairman
> Granada Television

The international coproduction business, which didn't even exist 10 years ago, emerged as one of the cornerstones of the new global television industry at the close of the '80s. Granada Television marched into the '90s with one of the most coveted prizes of coproduction's brief history: A coproduction with CBS Entertainment to produce six TV movies between 1991 and 1994. Each made-for-TV movie is budgeted at $4 million and will be shown in prime time on the ITV network in the United Kingdom and on CBS in America.

The final important cornerstone in the global television industry is international program sales. Added to the mega-mergers of international corporate giants and the emergence of international coproductions, international program sales form the three-part foundation of the new global television industry. Popular American programs like Dallas and The Cosby Show are distributed to television viewers in every corner of the world and are translated into dozens of different languages. The international selling of American programs hit the big time and emerged into a billion dollar-a-year industry during the '80s. International program sales had been a very small piece of the television pie until early in the decade. The major U.S. production/distribution companies had a small contingent of specialized, experienced salespeople who sold programs to the largely monopolistic government-protected stations throughout the world. But throughout the '80s in country after country, the monopolies gave way to open market economic policies. Television systems were deregulated and competition began in earnest. The new competition, primarily in Western Europe, created a tremendous demand for huge volumes of American programming. It also fueled a constant rise in per-episode prices as stations decided to outspend their competitors for the highly desirable U.S. shows. In Italy, for example, new competition sparked a 300 percent increase in license fees for some American programs. Deregulation in France drove the price of American programs up by over 100 percent. By the end of the '80s the competition for programming between BSB and Sky TV in the United Kingdom drove prices up by 100 percent. Finally, Spain, the last major European monopoly marketplace, set off a feeding frenzy for American programs in 1990 by licensing three new commercial stations.

Unfortunately, just as the American producers and distributors were becoming used to the exploding international market sales started to even out, and, in some cases, retreat, as the decade came to an end.

> Foreign [sales] looks good year-to-year as a given country
> opens up and becomes privatized. So, you get a surge in
> Italy. We made deals in Spain this year. Last year it was
> France. Germany is just tinkering around with opening up a
> little bit. You had the big fight going on down in Australia
> three years ago. Then, they all went bankrupt and now
> Australia is really consolidated. So, foreign for a while has
> really been up and down. It's usually been one country each
> year that's giving you the top spin. Set against that
> background is the fact that you have the common market
> coming into being and some pretty outrageous quota
> demands being put on the table which will, if passed, severely
> restrict American product flowing to these foreign countries,
> which might take away a lot of the economic underpinning of
> our deficit financing. So that's the marketplace that we're
> now working in.
>
> Rich Frank, President
> Walt Disney Studios

Throughout the '80s the dramatic increase in the number of networks and stations in Europe created a booming market for American programs. But, once the new stations had satisfied their needs for large volumes of programming with bulk purchases of American shows, purchasing patterns became much more selective. Even in the best of times, American programs were only worth a fraction of their domestic value in the non-U.S. markets. The Cosby Show reportedly sold for about $300,000 per episode in a single major U.S. market, while it fetched only $12,500 per episode in the entire United Kingdom.

Despite the fact that the boom days of international sales are over, American television programs are now a staple ingredient in the television diet of hundreds of millions of viewers in most countries of the world. Warner Brothers International, under the leadership of its international executive, Michael Solomon, is aggressively opening up the last few territories on the earth. Warner Bros. has negotiated a barter agreement with the Chinese television system. The hit American shows Hunter and Falcon Crest are shown each week in translated versions in four major Chinese provinces. The audience for these American programs—450 million per week!

> This is something that most people don't realize. Yes, we have increased the revenue base outside the United States. But, at the same time, that doesn't mean that necessarily it's translated into additional profits because network license fees in the United States have been reduced considerably. And, number two, the syndicated marketplace is overcrowded today and the amount of money that companies are making today in the syndicated market for off-network shows is not what it was five years ago. Therefore, the additional money that we are making overseas should never be construed by anybody as a windfall. I'm just saying this for the record. International revenue has actually replaced some domestic revenue.
>
> Michael Solomon, President
> Warner Bros. International

International selling of American programs now is settling in as one of the important marketing elements in the new global television industry. Even though the completion of deregulation in Europe has slowed down the volume of American programs sold, there is no denying that America is the primary creative force in global television. The '90s commenced with the announcement that Gosteleradio, the state television network of Russia, had purchased programming from MTV. Each Friday night, MTV-trained video jockeys host a one-hour music video program on the Vzglad youth program.

The '80s: A Review

During the 1980s three primary trends impacted the television industry. The mass audience was fragmented into smaller niche audiences. All of this came about as a result of satellite delivery of specialized cable networks, the growth of the independent station business, and the introduction of home video. It had a profound effect on advertising revenues and, thus, on traditional networks and their local affiliates.

Many of the industry's leading institutions were refinanced. The resulting pressure to contain expenses profoundly impacted the network and syndicated programming dimensions of the business.

Finally, during the '80s, the television industry became a global business with two-way pipelines for ideas and products extending to the farthest reaches of the globe.

Emerging trends of the '80s became the business realities of today. With this background knowledge serving as a foundation, our quest for insights into the future of television continues.

CHAPTER TWO

World
Television

Marshall McLuhan, the Canadian philosopher, may have been
the first to see it. Thirty years ago he prophesied the coming of
the information age; a time when instant electronic communication and traveling on yet-to-be-invented electronic transportation systems would turn the entire world, with all its oceans,
mountain ranges, and time zones, into one, compact global
village. The implications of McLuhan's vision were both dizzying and sobering. McLuhan's book, *Understanding Media*, was
hotly debated on campuses, in newspapers and magazines, and
within the television industry. The often quoted phrase, "The

medium is the message," became part of the industry's language, but only a few of those who used the phrase actually understood what it meant.

The Global Village

Like many people starting out in the television business in the '60's, I was instinctively attracted to the concept of the global village, but I did not really *see* it until I read a piece written by Les Brown in *Channels* magazine, at the end of 1987. In this piece, titled "The Path Once Taken," Brown outlined the most significant changes on the American television scene during the '80s. He wrote about the fractionalizing of the mass market, the growth of barter advertising, and the impact of the new economic realities on program production. He argued that the same essential forces were at work outside the United States. Finally, he concluded that the tools of the information age—computers, fax machines, and satellites—combined with affordable transatlantic airfares—insured that U.S.-style television would become the model for the rest of the world. In summary, his vision was challenging without being terribly threatening. "It may turn out that Europe's new commercial channels will feed heavily on old American series. But in exchange, U.S. networks and Hollywood studios may be building their futures on foreign coproduction. In the end, it should all resolve as world television, and that would be hard to dislike."

The speed with which television became globalized was phenomenal. As dramatic and as revolutionary as this change has been, for practical purposes it all happened in the last half of the 1980s. Every year new records are set for attendance at the major program conferences. At the largest, the NATPE conference held annually in January, the visitors guide booklet is now distributed in six different languages. At MIP and MIPCOM, advertisers, lawyers, accountants, and bankers from all over the world mingle with European, Asian, American, Latin, and Australian television executives. The discussions, conducted in a variety of the world's languages, are about buying and selling programs in previously closed markets. They are talking about program quotas, the cultural nationalism of various territories, and the impact of American programming on the world scene. Finally, their discussions include the financial consolidation of some of the big players and the delicate mechanics of international coproduction.

Reflecting the industry's fascination with the short- and long-term implications of globalization, seminars are now held in major world capitals throughout the year. One such seminar was held in Luxembourg in 1990. One of the opening speakers summarized the mixed feelings shared by many leaders of the European television community.

The theme of this conference reflected in this first session is the new global marketplace which the revolution in telecommunications has opened up for everyone involved in the media. Not only broadcasters, but bankers. Not only the advertising industry, but the investment industry. Not only the traditional broadcasting authorities, but the new breed of private broadcasting entrepreneurs.

All over the world the media frontiers are coming down. The old sacred frontier between telecommunications and broadcasting is disappearing. The broadcasting frontier that isolated Eastern Europe from the West has come down as dramatically as the Berlin Wall. The traditional frontier between European-style public service broadcasting and American-style commercial broadcasting is something of the past.

In that connection, we must try to ensure that as Europe's internal frontiers come down they are not replaced by an unnecessary new ''Berlin Wall'' of a fortress Europe. The new global market demands wisdom and self-restraint and give-and-take from the American media industry as well as inside Europe. There is the problem that the media hardware, the satellites and cables and encryption systems, are expanding much faster than the media software, the programs. If that imbalance is allowed to become too pronounced, it will be in nobody's interest, neither the investors, the advertisers, nor the viewers.

I sat in a home recently with the proud owner of a large satellite dish that could be moved from one orbital position to another at the touch of a remote control. We spent a happy hour zapping from one to another of around a hundred stations without ever stopping on one. It was a warning to me. We must try to avoid turning the global marketplace into a society of three-minute zappers. We can only do so by organizing internationally both program finance and structures for distribution that enable a diverse range of programs to be made which are compelling watching for the viewer.

Lord Thomson
Conference Chair
Luxembourg Media Summit
1990

The International Marketplace

Much of what American television executives think of as the international marketplace is composed of the five largest markets in Western Europe. In the United Kingdom, France, Italy, Spain, and Germany the television business has been turned upside-down over the past few years. One result of the turmoil has been that thousands of hours of American television programs have been sold to feed the appetite of new stations and networks. Now, as European trade barriers are beginning to come down and be replaced by a new free-trade common market approach, there are mixed views about the long-term health of the marketplace. A research report by Booze, Allen and Hamilton, in London, supports the position that the boom times will continue. The study concludes that revenues generated by the European broadcast, film, and home-video businesses could jump from $28 billion to $58 billion in the next 10 years. Booze, Allen predicts that nearly $15 billion of that increase will come from the growth of pay-TV, which is only in its infancy now. Further, East European markets are expected to jump on the commercial television bandwagon and generate nearly $7 billion by the turn of the century. With such large amounts of money at stake, Booze, Allen anticipates that over the next few years there will be significant changes in television ownership resulting from a series of mergers and acquisitions. They expect that the M & A activity will feature non-media firms which are eager to get into what they perceive to be a booming business, and traditional media firms which adopt a strategy of horizontal and vertical integration.

That relatively rosy forecast is in contrast to a report on media trends recently released by CIT, another London-based media research group. CIT speculates that the growth in total broadcast television hours in Western Europe will continue its spectacular rise through 1991. The CIT report also says growth will taper off dramatically during the rest of the decade. It also warns that more competition among broadcasters and program makers will result in more thinly spread revenues. An additional main thrust of the study is that despite the fast pace of deregulation and the commercialization of Europe's TV industry, the traditional, established public service broadcasters will remain the most popular with viewers for years to come.

Despite the somewhat conflicting predictions of the future of European television, one well-known industry leader has no doubt that Europeans will be watching more television.

The really big development that will occur in the '90s is that the rest of the world will be catching up with the multitude of formats that are occurring here in the United States—and that's already happening. Cable is going into Israel and direct satellite in Europe and Japan and so forth. And, there will be cable or DBS (Direct Broadcast Satellite) in Hong Kong. So the people will be getting more choices in other parts of the world and that always increases total television viewing. Here in the United States I don't think people will be watching significantly more television because it is inconceivable to me that there will be that many new networks with that many compelling new formats. I think all the major formats have already been developed.

Ted Turner
Chairman/Founder
Turner Broadcasting System

Societal Effects of World Television

From an audience and social point of view, the internationalization of the television industry is a major controversy. At the headquarters of the European Commission (EC) in Brussels the legislators argue and debate about what they call cultural nationalism. They threaten to impose quotas and regulations to prevent the Americanization of their cultures. Similar debates rage among the broadcasting authorities of the various European countries. France, in particular, seems worried and threatened by the potential of world television, particularly American, to degrade its cultural heritage. But, many proponents of world television feel that the market-driven nature of the business will insure that programming is balanced to reflect the interests of local audiences.

> I think the concept of global television is fast becoming a reality in terms of news, music, and sports. I think that on other fronts you'll see more crossing of lines but I don't think you'll see exactly a worldwide television market, one product serving all markets, because there are still major differences. Even in Western Europe you see regional differences not only by language but by region. There are definitely interest differences. But, there will be more properties crossing borders than you've ever seen and it will continue to happen. U.S.A. Network is going to be televising the World League of Football, which is a spring league that plays in four European cities. It's an effort to export American football to a new audience. I think some of these things will develop with some degree of success. You're going to see in the United States some distribution of product that is produced for places that are foreign to the United States but that will have some level of interest in the United States. That has never happened before other than the fact that for years British television has exported programs to the United States for PBS. Other than that, it has not really existed in the United States. I think you will see that in the next ten years.

> Kay Koplovitz
> President
> U.S.A. Network

The impact of global television on the people of the world is a fascinating topic of discussion, but scientists and researchers have just begun to study the subject and very little is really known about it.

In the short term, in many cases, globalization is going to force dislocations that are problematic. When I was in Russia I talked to a girl just out of college. I said, ''How is it different now than it was two years ago?'' She said that it's much more depressing. I said, ''Why? Look at all the things you can do.'' And she said, ''Now I know that I know everything about my life. I know that I will never have an apartment, that I will always live with my parents. Or, when I get married I will live with my husband's parents because I know there are not enough apartments in Moscow. And, I know all about the food shortages and everything else.'' So, I think that's a temporary dislocation because if she now knows and if eventually everybody will know, then they'll push to change it. But, it's interesting to hear that kind of a viewpoint on things. Knowledge can be a depressing factor at any moment.

Rich Frank
President
Walt Disney Studios

Consolidation and Coproduction

The consolidation of financial power and the coproduction of programming are the two final pieces of the puzzle that make the new business called ''World Television.'' In the United States, the financial winds of change have largely come from the Far East. The stunning acquisitions of Columbia by Sony, and MCA by Matsushita, swept through the financial communities leaving behind a vastly altered business landscape. The combination of Time and Warner created the world's most powerful media enterprise; a company whose influence and leverage is unparalleled in business history. Among the many and far-reaching effects of global financial consolidation is a determined effort by the big three U.S. networks to unshackle themselves from the government regulations that prevent them from becoming major players in the new world of global television.

For twenty years, the so-called "Fyn-Syn" (financial-syndication) rules have restricted the networks from owning companies that make and syndicate television programming. Once the Federal Communications Commission drops or softens these rules, many financial analysts predict a consolidation of major Hollywood studios and one or more of the big three networks. This approach would automatically put a network in a front seat position in the new global television marketplace. The networks want to compete in the new game so badly that they have significantly intensified their lobbying efforts in Washington and are waging a vocal public relations war. As Matsushita completed its purchase of MCA for more than $6 billion at the end of 1990, Bob Wright, chairman of NBC, was quoted in *Business Week* as saying: "A global cartel is developing which threatens the existence of America's independent producers."

Europe has also been experiencing a consolidation of financial power in recent years that most analysts predict will continue. They eagerly await the final auctioning of the ITV franchises in the United Kingdom and predict that the most startling merger and acquisition activity in the history of the European media business will result.

Financial competition in the European television markets has already become very serious. Some industry leaders think that the most dramatic developments are just around the corner.

> Different things are going to happen in different places. Take the United Kingdom, where we have a very regulated system, in essence a monopoly on advertising time that will last another two or three years. I think there are various changes that one can see happening. First, we're going to have to get used to a very strange notion that we have all gotten familiar with in other media, and that is that the era of the unsuccessful television company hasn't really occurred yet in Europe. Television companies have uniformly and universally been successful.
>
> The fact is that the number of TV channels that are opening up and the growth in the number of channels is far

in excess of the growth of the amount of advertising money. And, so, the stations are going to find it difficult to buy high quality programs and for some of them even to survive. Because, without the high quality programs or without highly rated programming they won't get the audiences and, if they don't get the audiences, they won't get the advertising. So, a vicious circle continues. I think we'll see the beginning of an era of unsuccessful TV stations, just as in the same way, for many years, we have seen unsuccessful magazines, unsuccessful radio stations, and unsuccessful newspapers. I think we'll have to get used to the fact that TV can also be unsuccessful.

> Brian Jacobs
> Vice-Chairman
> Leo Burnett Limited, London

Warnings about the pitfalls of moving from a protected marketplace to a free-market, competitive marketplace come from many sectors, including the banking industry.

Heightened level of competition has eroded the value of any single franchise. The growth in opportunity that people perceive means that competition will increase. Managers who are sensitive to the marketplace as well as the cost of providing programming will succeed, and the others will fail. Success is no longer preordained. The difficulty of judging public taste and making forward financial commitments places a premium on management. There is a growing analogy with the radio industry in America. In large radio markets in America with as many as 80 to 100 signals, a significant number of stations are unprofitable at any one point in time. Having only 5 percent to 6 percent of the audience may give you the number-one position. The market leader may change year to year, depending upon the public taste and imitators who have easy access. It is important to know the market leader is not necessarily the most profitable station and in some instances may make relatively little money. Television is much less fragmented. But, the necessity to acquire programming well in advance of its use increases financial risk substantially. While radio is more fragmented, it also has lower programming costs and therefore is more adaptable. Lower margins and returns on equity have been the trend in network for the past five years. This will continue. Tom Murphy [Chairman, CapCities/ABC] has said to me that running a network is worse than banking.

> Thomas Reifenheiser
> Senior Vice President
> The Chase Manhattan Bank

The concept of program coproduction was born out of economic need. The businesses that use programs—stations, networks, and distributors—can lower the cost of acquiring material by sharing the expense with other users. Nearly all the major players agree that program coproduction is a mandatory reality of television life in the '90s. But few coproductions end up as marriages made in heaven. Many problems, in both the creative and financial sense, plague the coproduction business. Most experts feel that these problems will be overcome throughout the decade because the business has no other choice.

> The most likely outcome is that there will be increased partnerships between major companies, and major companies and minor companies, who will find both financial and operational justifications for joint ventures. They will have to pursue joint ventures because the marketplace will not tolerate large acquisitions that will substantially dilute earnings. And, I think, more importantly, those joint ventures are likely to take the form of rather than simply cash purchases of a 50 percent interest in businesses, people will combine businesses without direct cash exchanges, in effect, bartering companies where there is a perceived benefit in having those companies under the same umbrella. The one positive development I see from all this, in effect, increasing global joint venture process, is that as these partnerships begin to develop, there will be further global political pressure, and, hopefully, economic logic, to reduce some of the existing regulatory barriers that I, for one, don't quite

understand. And hopefully, as those barriers begin to break down that will re-encourage growth, more traditional forms of growth in the entertainment and broadcasting environment.

Fred Seegal
Managing Director
Shearson Lehman Hutton Inc.

The internationalization of the television business is a contemporary trend that portends the future of the industry. World television involves the introduction of competition in major markets that traditionally operated as monopolies. It involves the emergence of global lifestyles as experienced by a new, internationally conscious television audience. And, it involves the merging of international business interests, both financially and creatively.

CHAPTER THREE

The United Kingdom

The '90s promise sweeping, revolutionary changes for the once peaceful British television business. Although it is impossible to predict what the television landscape will look like by the turn of the century, it is certain that what happens in the United Kingdom over the next several years will significantly affect the global television industry.

The Market

There are four primary television networks in the United Kingdom: BBC 1, BBC 2, ITV (composed of 15 regional stations), and Channel 4. *B-SKY-B* is the only satellite program service, beaming six channels to cable systems and home-mounted satellite dishes. Cable penetration is only 17 percent and 65 percent of the households have VCRs. Coronation Street, a twice-weekly soap opera, is the hottest domestic show. Father Dowling Investigates is the most popular American program in the United Kingdom's 21 million television households.

In the world television marketplace, the United Kingdom is a major player. Nearly $400 million is spent per year to purchase television programs from outside the country. Of that figure, 90 percent is spent on American-made product. The British are also among the most prolific contributors to international coproductions, having long-term coproduction alliances with broadcasters around the globe.

Although Mrs. Thatcher is no longer prime minister, the legacy of the Thatcher years is a powerful influence on the British television business.

One of the last major pieces of legislation passed during Thatcher's tenure is the controversial broadcasting bill that promises to deregulate the country's television industry. Industry leaders in Britain take great pride in the programs they have produced over the last fifty years. The specter of government-mandated "deregulation" is not eagerly anticipated.

> I can't, myself, project anything about the turn of the century in television without addressing what, for me, is the fundamental question. What is television for? Is it an entertainment medium? Is it going to be an informational technology medium? Or, is it going to increasingly be a medium that sells goods? And, if it is, then you're getting into the three-minute zappers culture, the best example of which is the United States. I think that you have to ask yourself if you think that TV has some duty to be a medium of information, to occasionally entertain, to illuminate, dare I say, inspire, in what it does. Then, I don't believe that can be achieved without some sort of regulation of the volume of channels that are going to be used. If not, the nation generally is going to be starved of some of the culture that television can provide for many of the people who do not seek the culture in more conventional manners. Howard Stringer was over from

CBS. He was speaking at a Royal TV Society lecture and he was talking at a time when the United Kingdom was still wrestling with its broadcasting bill. His warning was that there is so much choice and competition in the United States that no one any more watched a television program from its beginning to its end. That's probably a slight exaggeration. But, it's something with which I sympathize.

David Plowright
Chairman
Granada Television

The Broadcasting Act paved the way for the lucrative ITV franchises to be awarded, for a ten-year period in a sealed-bid auction process, beginning in 1993. It not only opens up the possibility that at least some of the 16 franchises will be "won" by new companies, it also opens the doors to mergers and take-overs in what, up until now, has been the cozy, collegial world of government-protected commercial broadcasting. This lottery has shocked the commercial broadcasting establishment which, over the years, has produced some of the world's best television including Brideshead Revisited and Jewel in the Crown. The rules of the lottery required that an applicant first demonstrate how it will provide a quality program service. Then, the applicant had to make a financial bid on the particular ITV regional license which it was trying to acquire. Financial analysts agreed that it was impossible to know what the value of an ITV license might be two or three years from now, let alone ten years down the road. The government has also announced that it will license a new channel in 1993. If such a channel were launched, it would surely affect the revenues of the ITV stations. Similarly, there is really no way to know what the long-term impact of B-SKY-B, the satellite service, will be on the ITV revenue stream. And, just to make the exercise a little more interesting, as the United Kingdom begins the '90s it finds itself in a financial recession. Inflation is about 10 percent and total expenditures for advertising on television are declining. Nonetheless, ITV stations are not put on the auction block every day. So, a variety of serious bidders made offers, including media giants from Italy, France, and the United States. Many in Britain's broadcasting establishment fear that by awarding the ITV franchises to the highest bidder, operators will have to assume enormous financial debt. The pressure to meet the obligations of that debt will then force the new operators to maximize profits by lowering expenses (laying off workers), and by maximizing revenues with the highest rated (lowest common denominator) programs. That reality, the establishment fears, will forever transform the British commercial broadcasting business from one that was driven by program excellence into one that is driven by profits.

> All of us making our ten-year forecasts, as we're obliged to do to make these bids, look at the possible decline in advertising revenues, and say: How do major companies continue to deliver growth to the bottom line in these circumstances when the traditional source of revenue is decreasing? Then people begin to think of other ways. So you increase your revenue by what we're doing a bit of in the international marketplace (coproductions and distribution). And at the same time you begin to ask yourself: Can you bid for a contract other than one? So, if you ask me to predict what the ITV system will be like in the year 2000 I do not think it will be the same structure of 15 independent companies operating the way they have. I think it's very likely that will be the system up until 1992. But, after that, there will be voluntary mergers, hostile takeovers, and what had been 15 independent ITV companies will probably become six or eight.
>
> David Plowright
> Chairman
> Granada Television

B-SKY-B

In contrast to the alarming and unpredictable prospects of revolutionary change faced by the commercial ITV companies, Rupert Murdoch's Sky Television, now commonly referred to as *B-SKY-B*, has emerged victorious from his direct-broadcast satellite (DBS) battle with British Satellite Broadcasting Company and is poised to become a major player in the U.K. television market. Murdoch and his competitors lost hundreds of millions in their efforts to launch financially viable DBS systems. When Sky TV and BSB merged at the end of 1990, it was clear that Murdoch was the winner, retaining 50 percent ownership of *B-SKY-B*. The former owners of BSB are now minority owners of the newly merged company. Murdoch has worked out a restructuring of debt for his umbrella company, News Corp., and is now poised to build viewership and revenues for *B-SKY-B* at the expense of the ITV stations and the BBC.

Murdoch's victory came after a competitive battle that was really about the question of the future of British television. At the Edinburgh TV festival in the summer of 1989 Murdoch drew first blood with a speech forecasting the end of the traditional British broadcasting world. He was quoted in *Television Business International (TBI)*.

> The arguments which have recently dominated British broadcasting, such as multi-channel choice versus public service duopoly, will soon sound as if they belong to the Stone Age. Much of what is claimed to be quality television here is no more than the parading of the prejudices and interests of the like-minded people who currently control British television. This public-service TV system has had, in my view, debilitating effects on British society, by producing a TV output which is so often obsessed with class, dominated by anti-commercial attitudes, and, with a tendency to hark back to the past.
>
> Rupert Murdoch
> *TBI*
> February 1990

Rupert Murdoch may have received, as reported, "warm applause." But he also inspired his competitors at BSB to concentrate their effort to beat Murdoch in the race to establish what nearly everyone in the business predicted would be the single surviving British DBS service.

> The reason BSB will succeed financially is that we see ourselves as part of the British television system. We set out to add to what BBC, ITV, and Channel 4 are doing. We do

not need to build our foundations on their ruins. If I may be allowed one remark about Mr. Murdoch's Sky Television it would be to draw this contrast. Mr. Murdoch has done extremely well. He has successfully launched four new television services, parts of which, most notably Sky News, are excellent. His newspaper business has played a very influential role in this achievement, from around the world supplying the news channel: in the U.K. creating an editorial groundswell against the four terrestrial channels, and then, of course, using the newspapers as promotional vehicles to sell receiving equipment direct to the customer. But the contrast is this: Mr. Murdoch says he does not respect British television. He seeks to replace it rather than complement it.

> Anthony Simonds-Gooding
> Former Chairman
> BSB

Five months after I heard Simonds-Gooding make his speech at the Luxembourg Media Summit, he was packing his bags and vacating his office at BSB headquarters. The owners of BSB apparently came to feel that competing against Rupert Murdoch and Sky TV was a losing proposition. *B-SKY-B* now has the entire satellite-to-home business to itself and will spend the rest of the decade exploiting its position in the market and maximizing its profits. With *B-SKY-B* in the United Kingdom; Newspapers in Australia, the United States and the United Kingdom; and the Fox company in the United States, which includes movies and television; Rupert Murdoch is well on his way to creating the world's first global entertainment, publishing, and television empire. During an interview with Murdoch, I asked him what was the most exciting opportunity on the horizon for his company over the next decade.

> Well, as I look forward, we are trying to build Sky TV and we're trying to build Fox TV. If we can do that, that will be plenty for one lifetime.

> Rupert Murdoch
> Chairman
> News Corporation

Public Service Broadcasting-The BBC

England's venerable public service network, the BBC, is not immune from the winds of change sweeping across the United Kingdom landscape. It faces arguments that its ratings do not justify its price (each television set in the country is taxed about $130 per year to pay for the BBC service). In 1996 the BBC's charter is up for renewal by the government. Beginning in 1993, a government review body will commence the debate over how and to what degree to fund the BBC in the future. The BBC is the standard by which public service broadcasting throughout the world is measured. I recently heard its director general outline the BBC's official mission.

> The BBC approaches its task from four perspectives. First, its responsibility to viewers and listeners. They pay their money for a broadcasting service of variety, range, and quality. Secondly, the BBC has a special responsibility to nurture public service broadcasting. It's an odd beast to define but its essence is broadcasting solely for the benefit of the viewers and listeners—the public rather than advertisers, the government, shareholders, and so on. Thirdly, to ensure that we go on meeting those other two responsibilities, we have a duty to plan ahead, to look at what the next few years will bring; years of considerable challenge—commercial and political—and chart a course for the corporation. Fourthly, we also have to encourage, support, and enthuse our 28,000 staff and manage a budget of over a billion pounds in a responsible, effective, and accountable way.
>
> Michael Checkland
> Director General
> BBC

Checkland recently gave some insight into the practical meaning of the phrase "chart a course for the corporation" when he announced that the BBC plans to take on Cable News Network (CNN) and launch a new international TV news service. The

BBC will offer its news programming service to broadcasters throughout the world. The new service is in the beginning stages of development and will build on its existing foundation of news-gathering capability. Checkland has not announced a specific launch date for the service but he indicated it would be early in the 1990s.

The increasingly competitive nature of British broadcasting and the recessionary economy are working together to keep the pressure on the BBC to be more market-sensitive and cost effective. Already, the approved budget through 1993 has been cut by $150 million, and millions of dollars worth of capital improvements have been shelved. The director general has announced that nearly 4,000 jobs will be eliminated by 1993. Even plans for a new $285 million London headquarters building have been postponed. In what is surely a sign of the times, the BBC says it will use the money to buy and to make programs which will compete more aggressively with ITV and *B-SKY-B*.

Britain's program production business went into a slump in the later half of the '80s. The government has now mandated that the BBC, as well as other British broadcasters, must purchase 25 percent of their required programming from independent producers.

> We have a really extraordinary system here in the United Kingdom which Americans never believe, but, which, believe me, is true, about who actually owns the programs. If you're an independent production company in the United Kingdom and you make a program, the program is actually owned by the broadcaster, not by you. If you are commissioned you do not, as in the United States, rent your program to the broadcaster for a period of, say five years, and then you get it back again and create a secondary market. That doesn't happen here because the show is forever owned by the broadcaster. So, therefore, there is no secondary market and there are no independent producers selling away their souls, as it were, to the broadcasters. That will also, I suspect, change because we now have a pretty flourishing and pretty new independent production industry growing up. The so-called 25 percent lobby is, I think, one of the most extraordinary lobbying achievements in recorded time. I

mean these guys came from nowhere and they've suddenly got 25 percent of broadcasting. So, that's another change where a greater supply of programming from wherever, be it the independent sector, be it advertisers, be it sponsored programs or cofunded programs, or whatever. All these things are starting to emerge and will emerge at a greater pace over the next several years.

> Brian Jacobs
> Vice-Chairman
> Leo Burnett Limited, London

With a significant amount of its programming mandated to come from independent producers, with its funding from taxes levied on television set owners under constant scrutiny, and with ITV, *B-SKY-B*, and cable television threatening to reduce its viewership, the BBC faces a challenging decade, to use some classic British understatement. The British television experience in the '90s will likely pit two completely different business philosophies in head-to-head competition for the viewers' attention. On the one side is the *B-SKY-B* approach: "give em' what they want." On the other side is the BBC approach: "give em' what they need." The eyes of the world's television community will watch and await the outcome.

Cable TV

Cable television has been slow to develop in Britain. It currently has less than 20 percent penetration into television households. Whether it will become a competitive medium during the '90s depends on whether or not the mostly-American companies are willing and able to make the extraordinary investment required to build the infrastructure.

> The difficulty in cable is in laying the wire which will permit interactivity and laying them in a discreet, conservation-minded manner rather than doing what you've done, which is stretching wires all over the United States. That's one of the reasons why cable hasn't worked in the United Kingdom.

If we had been allowed to put them on the telegraph poles and just run the cables then it would have happened quicker. But the costs of digging trenches and burying them have, so far, prohibited them. But I've no doubt signs are there even in the United Kingdom that telephone companies in the United States are not looking for a short-term payback on cable. They are saying that they are beginning to look at interactive cable systems in the United Kingdom over a ten-year period. And, they are saying: I'm going to pay my debt and I'm prepared to invest. They haven't done it yet. But they say they are going to do it.

> David Plowright
> Chairman
> Granada Television

A number of American companies have been awarded franchises to build cable systems in the United Kingdom. They include United Artists Entertainment, COMCAST, U.S. West, Jones Intercable, and Pacific Telesis. But with economic recessions afflicting both sides of the Atlantic at the beginning of the decade, and with *B-SKY-B*'s head start in the direct satellite broadcasting business, the jury is still out on whether cable will emerge into a major player in British television. One study, by Edelman Public Relations Worldwide, in 1991, projected that British cable penetration would jump to nearly 30 percent by the middle of the 1990s.

The Future

Despite the turmoil in their domestic marketplace, the British are aggressively staking out an important position in the world television business.

- Granada Television is coproducing eight made-for-television movies for HBO and six more for CBS Entertainment. It has also put together two major production coventures without American partners. One involves the production of movies with German network, NDR, and

Hachette International, in France. The other involves the ZDF network in Germany for the coproduction of dramatic programs in English.

- The BBC has entered into an international comedy development deal with CBS. A BBC-produced comedy series aired in America, on CBS, in the summer of 1991. The BBC also coproduces with the Arts and Entertainment cable network in the United States as well as several stations in the American PBS system.

- On the continent, the BBC is coproducing three miniseries with Reteitalia, in Italy. Their first joint project with the Burlusconi company is an adaptation of Lady Chatterley's Lover.

- Yorkshire TV has set up a coventure with NBC to develop European projects which will air on the American network.

- Thames TV, the largest ITV broadcaster, has acquired New York-based Reeves Entertainment to strengthen its position in the United States.

- TVS Entertainment, another major ITV company, is also the owner of the famous Los Angeles-based television producer, MTM.

- Central TV owns 49 percent of Chris Beard Entertainment, the U.S. producer of The Gong Show and Puttin on the Hits.

- Finally, Channel 4 is coproducing a comedy show with an American production company for the U.S. cable network, The Comedy Channel.

The British television industry approaches the year 2000 with a rich tradition of excellent television productions and with its traditional ways of doing business under attack on many fronts. During the '90s Britain's television leaders will maneuver for position in an increasingly competitive environment, and they will devote more and more energy to solidifying their strong position as producers for world television.

CHAPTER FOUR

France

At the dawn of the '90s, most of the French television business found itself mired in debt and suffering under the burden of government interference. This surprising development came only three years after the French market was generally considered one of the hottest in Europe. Despite these problems, and no compelling reason to think the market situation will improve dramatically any time soon, several French companies are poised to become major players on the world television scene.

The Market

France has 20 million television homes. There are three private commercial networks: TF-1, La Cinq, and M-6. These channels, plus the three public-service channels—Antenne 2, FR-3, and La Sept—are all supported in part by license fees paid by television consumers. Canal Plus is an over-the-air pay-TV service, which, ironically, is the most successful and profitable television service in Europe.

Television viewing in France is not as prevalent as it is in the United States. The average Frenchman watches about three hours of TV a day. TF-1 dominates the market. It has nearly twice the audience of its nearest rival. Occasionally one of the public-service channels will score higher ratings, but TF-1's program schedule features the country's most popular programs which include French feature films, the police action-adventure series Navarro and French variety shows. Knots Landing and Santa Barbara are the hottest U.S.-made TV shows. American blockbuster movies also do very well on French television. There is one final market statistic which may portend the future: American programs do much better with children aged 11–14 than they do with the general audience. Within the French audience of tomorrow, five of the top ten programs are American. Cable penetration is only about 19 percent while about 40 percent of the television households have VCRs.

Public Service Broadcasting

A few years ago, France had three state-controlled public-service broadcasters, and 90 percent of the programming was produced in France. Then, in 1986, the Socialist party authorized two new private commercial networks: La Cinq and M-6. International distributors, particularly Americans, envisioned the birth of a major competitive marketplace. They sold hundreds of hours of American programs to the new stations and, nearly overnight, the so-called international boom was born. Then, there was an amazing political development. Jacques Chirac, a conservative, was elected prime minister of France on a political platform that included a promise to cancel the franchises of La Cinq and M-6, while simultaneously privatizing and commercializing TF-1. The result was chaos. Overnight, TF-1 became the market leader, controlling the popular programming and the huge majority of the market's advertising. The promise of an audience-driven, competitive market evaporated. Then, everything changed *again* when Chirac lost his campaign to become the president of France. The Socialists came back to power. They put the two new commercial networks back in business and promised to let the broadcasting industry settle down. By the beginning of the '90s TF-1 was marginally profitable, the other networks had lost hundreds of millions of dollars, and the government had imposed program quotas and various other operational regulations. The international boom was over and the French television industry was in a tailspin.

Programmers at the French networks essentially program to satisfy the requirements of government regulators rather than television viewers. Fifty percent of film and fiction programming must be French language production, while 60 percent must be European-made. No network can show more than 192 films per year. Only 104 of those can air in prime time before 10:30 P.M., and movies cannot be shown on Wednesday, Friday, or Saturday nights. Advertising is limited to six minutes per hour. Films can only be interrupted once. Time for political candidates is regulated. Certain films require warnings about their content and their scheduling time is restricted. The networks are all required to turn part of their income over to French television producers.

Given what has happened in the last few years in French television, experts are at a loss to predict the future. All that can be said is that the current situation, with nearly everyone in the business losing money, cannot last long. The leaders of the French TV industry and the French politicians are left to find solutions.

A new quota rule is in the works. Reportedly, the rule that forces producers to shoot programs from an original French script will be changed so that producers can shoot from a script originally written in any language as long as French is used by the actors. The rule requiring networks to broadcast 120 hours per year of original French fiction will be broadened to allow the networks to air 120 hours of *European* fiction. Finally, the president of the public-service networks, Hervé Bourges, has a plan that will merge Antenne 2 and FR-3 into one company that operates two networks, very much like BBC-1 and BBC-2 in England. He hopes that the efficiencies achieved through this approach will help the stations become financially stable. He has quite a job facing him. In 1990, Antenne 2 and FR-3 together lost more than $150 million.

Cable TV

The future of the French cable industry is equally puzzling. The government launched a plan in 1982 promising to pass five million French households with fiber-optic cable by 1987. Nine years after the cable plan was launched, only 2.5 million homes had been passed, and coaxial cable had replaced the fiber-optics. Several new cable networks have recently been launched, but building of the infrastructure is slow and whether cable will be able to build the revenue momentum to challenge the terrestrial networks—and pay-TV giant, Canal + —is, at best, an unanswered question.

While government interference seems to have severely retarded the growth of broadcasting and cable in France, one French company, which was actually created by the government in 1984, has become Europe's most successful television company.

We have to thank the French regulation. It's not just a joke. In the beginning of Canal + we were obliged to build a service called Canal + based on theatrical movies. But because of the goverment regulations at the time, we were only allowed to broadcast theatrical movies 45 percent of the time.

We had to create 55 percent of our schedule. So we tried to find several strategies which were very simple for the subscriber to identify. So now we are 45 percent movies, 7 percent live sports events, 15 percent made-for-television movies, and lots of documentaries and specials. Sometimes we do inquiries or investigations but not on a regular basis; when we have a good subject like money or drugs we use them. We also have a lot of children's programs, and we have two unscrambled periods, at lunch time and dinner time. Mostly they are music and talk shows. Why those two windows? Because of the French regulations. We started in the first years of the Socialist party. There was a big fight between the majority and the opposition. The opposition said: "Wow, what a stupid idea. The Socialists have created pay-TV. The world is tumbling down. That is TV for the rich people." So, the Socialists told us: "You have to keep

free a little window in a good popular time slot.'' So, we said
OK: at lunch time and dinner time. So, we said: OK.
During those slots we have to be free. So, we talk to the
people, even those who are not our subscribers, and we show
them what we are and we do lots of promotions. That was
the story. That was to explain to you that we are not
geniuses. We were responding to the government regulations.

Now we have the deep conviction that in a country big
enough to amortize an important investment in terms of
programs and marketing you can have a special format
halfway between thematic and network.

> Pierre Lescure
> CEO
> Canal +

The success of Canal + became legendary within a few years.
It has three million paying subscribers, is not dependent on
ratings or advertisers, has expanded into a variety of other markets, and earned about $225 million in profits in 1991.

Canal + is emerging as a dynamic player in the world television business. Its rapidly expanding interests include:

- minority ownership of Canal + channels in Belgium,
  Spain, and Germany.

- 10 percent ownership of TVS, one of the ITV stations
  in the United Kingdom.

- 5 percent of Carolco Entertainment in Los Angeles.

- 28 percent of TV-Sport, a French satellite sports channel.

- 30 percent of Sportkanal, a German satellite sports operation.

- 10 percent of the Dutch sports network, Sportnet.

Finally, in early 1991, the company announced the creation of
Studio Canal + , which is expected to finance between $50–$100
million in film production in its first year of operation.

Canal + is clearly committed to establishing a major French presence in the international television business. Its accomplishments up until now may be dwarfed by its performance during the '90s. By the end of 1991, Canal + hopes to launch the first pay-TV service in Russia!

Coproduction

Although the French production business starts the new decade as a victim of that country's struggling television industry, the lure of profits from the international marketplace continues to attract producers to the French coproduction arena.

At least four major American companies have investments and coproduction arrangements with French producers.

- The Hearst Corporation owns 20 percent of Elipse, which is one-third owned by Canal + .

- Group W Television owns 50 percent of a new venture called Futurimages.

- Time–Warner owns 20 percent of Initial Groupe, which was originally purchased by Telepictures.

- Finally, ABC is a 25 percent owner of Hamster, France's biggest and most successful production company.

Hamster, founded 20 years ago by Pierre Grimblat, has a catalog of over 250 productions and produces over 20 percent of all the French movies shown on prime-time television. The company expects its relationship with ABC to make it a major player in global coproductions. It is also starting up a development group to produce sitcoms and soap operas.

The Future

French television programs have rarely found audience acceptance in other parts of the world, but a number of leaders in the

French TV industry are committed to carving out a piece of the international television pie. In 1990, a communications consulting firm, Paris Globe, staged the first Paris screenings. Designed to be similar to the annual British and German screenings, the Paris screenings bring in program buyers from throughout the world. It is hoped that, over time, a secondary marketplace for French programs will develop. A promising development occurred in late 1991 when a sitcom, called The Ramdam Family, which airs on M-6, was sold to the Dutch and Swedish public television services. In the meantime, French involvement in the international television community of the '90s will depend largely on the activities of Canal + and the American-backed production companies.

CHAPTER FIVE

Italy

The Italian television business, which has often been described as the Wild West of European broadcasting, begins the 1990s with a new broadcasting law that promises to stabilize what has often been an extremely volatile marketplace. The state-owned RAI networks and the three privately owned Burlusconi networks will share the vast majority of the profits of what amounts to a government-regulated duopoly. During the next decade, experts predict a reduction in the amount of American product purchased by Italian television buyers, an increase in the amount of coproduction, and the global expansion of Silvio Burlusconi's media empire.

The Market

Italy is the most mature television market in Europe. Its twenty million viewers are exposed to an astounding number of over-the-air television signals. There are nearly 1,400 privately owned local stations. They complement the three state-owned RAI networks: RAI-1, RAI-2 and RAI-3. The television landscape is rounded out by the three Burlusconi-owned Reteitalia network stations: Canale-5, Italia Uno, and Rete-4. There is virtually no cable television in Italy and VCRs are in only about 35 percent of the television households. RAI, the number-one network, and Reteitalia, number two, together split about 90 percent of the approximately $1.7 billion spent annually on television advertising.

Watching television is a very popular pastime in Italy. The most popular programs are Italian mini-series and local variety programs. Twin Peaks was recently the highest rated American program.

Italy was the first European marketplace to deregulate its television industry. In the late 1970s, private television was authorized and hundreds and hundreds of local stations began broadcasting. The advertising market was very small so, to survive, many stations sold their airtime to local programmers and to home-shopping advertisers. This led to some of the most bizarre programming and advertising ever seen anywhere on television. By the mid-'80s, Silvio Burlusconi, a Milan-based real estate entrepreneur, had emerged as the major player in the new commercial television industry. He established a chain of stations in all the major population centers and then circumvented the law that prohibited a private national network. By sending videotapes of his programs to his various stations and then requiring them all to be aired at the same time throughout the country he broke the advertising monopoly of the state-owned networks. Competition for U.S. programs between RAI and Reteitalia during the '80s was one of the main contributors to what eventually became known in America as the international boom. U.S. programmers sold the two competing networks hundreds of millions of dollars worth of American-made productions.

Now that the new government broadcasting laws essentially guarantee an advertising duopoly, both RAI and Reteitalia have announced that they will reduce the amount of their American-made program purchases and concentrate their energies on servicing the debt they incurred during the competitive licensing wars of the '80s.

RAI

The giant Italian public broadcaster, RAI, was founded in the 1920s when Benito Mussolini ruled the country. In 1955 it began television broadcasting. Today it runs six national radio networks, three national television networks, and employs over 13,000 people. RAI's baptism into the world of competition during the '80s was hard-fought and expensive. The company's top managers describe their strategy for the '90s as conservative and austere. The amount of American television programs purchased will go down. One reason for this projection is that when all is said and done, Italians like Italian programs most. Also, the new broadcasting law requires that 40 percent of the movies airing on network television must be produced in the European Community.

Throughout the '90s, RAI will continue to be a major coproducer of television programs for the global marketplace. RAI is coproducing a new big-budget television series called Foreign Correspondent with Los Angeles-based Spectator Films. The story involves an American newsman, based in Rome, who covers news events throughout Europe.

RAI is coproducing made-for-TV movies with the U.S.A. Network. It is involved in a major coproduction with a consortium of French, German, and U.K. companies, and it has coproduced a program on the life of Michelangelo with Turner Broadcasting.

Reteitalia

Silvio Burlusconi reportedly got his start in the television business by opening a station in an apartment in a residential section of Milan in the mid-'70s. Today, Silvio Burlusconi Communications is one of Europe's biggest and strongest media empires. In addition to the three Reteitalia commercial networks and dozens of other companies, Burlusconi owns a chain of movie theaters, a film production and distribution company, a significant percentage of television networks in France, Spain, and Germany, 10 percent of Italy's first pay-TV company, a media rep firm, and a highly successful professional soccer team. Burlusconi, a consummate showman and one of Europe's highest-profile businessmen, is poised to become one of the most important players in the global television industry.

Burlusconi's strategy for his network stations in the '90s includes a reduction in the amount of American-made movies. He will increase the amount of Italian-produced mini-series and expand the broadcast of live sports, news, and variety programming.

Part of his strategy is in response to the new government regulations mandating that 40 percent of the movies shown on television be European-made, and that movies only be interrupted once for commercials. It is the dimension of the new regulations that controls programming which some American producers and distributors find so confusing and frustrating.

> In an animated series you're not allowed any breaks. That's just an example of government fighting back, being afraid of a free market. It has a devastating impact on Burlusconi. I have a tremendous number of animated programs. Well, he may be hesitant now in buying animated programs. The government is stupid because the government is essentially saying: "We don't want commercials in animation." So, what will Burlusconi do? He won't buy animation because his is a private company which depends on profit. And how's he going to make a profit if he can't sell commercials? So, what the government is doing is essentially, at the end of the day, denying children animated programs. So, what do you gain from that?

> Michael Solomon
> President
> Warner Bros. International

Reteitalia is a major player in the international coproduction business. It is producing a prime-time, four-hour, mini-series with Beta Tarus in Germany. An $18-million movie called The Burning Shore has been shot in several locations as a coproduction with Germany's Beta Tarus and France's TF-1. Another Beta Tarus coproduction, The Lion of the Desert, has been shot in New York. During 1990 alone, Reteitalia was involved in coproductions exceeding 120 hours of television programming. Recently, Burlusconi and HBO launched a very complicated $20-million coproduction. Shot on location, Mother Russia will use European and American actors and will end up as a 10-hour mini-series. And, in what is probably a first for American television, a Reteitalia-created and produced game show is scheduled to be offered in U.S. syndication. The Italian prime-time hit C'Eravamo Tanto Amati will be turned into an English language program called We Loved Each Other So Much. Couples appear on the show and try to persuade the audience to take sides in an actual long-standing fight. Each spouse brings a witness to testify on his or her behalf. The tone is confrontational and argumentative, and the audience ultimately votes a winner. Many Italian television critics have apparently panned the show as setting a new low in bad taste, but few would be willing to take a bet that it won't become a ratings hit in the United States!

The scope of Silvio Burlusconi's ambitions for his company have been revealed by his reported plan to make public 40 percent of his company on the Milan and New York stock exchanges. The capital generated by such a move would be used to finance expansion into the East European countries and the Soviet Union.

Pay-TV

Experts predict that the final piece of the '90s puzzle is the birth of pay-TV in Italy. Silvio Burlusconi, who is now barred from controlling a pay-TV company by the new government regulations, has launched Tele PIU-1. He has already sold 90 percent of the company to a group of Italian investors with whom he has a variety of business interests. It already has 100,000 subscribers and is projected to have over one million by the end of 1993. For a fee of $28 a month, Tele PIU-1 subscribers receive about 120 movies, 25 of which are television premiers. Until recently it was thought that pay-TV would not work in Italy because viewers already had so many options that they would reject paying for more. But, the new government regulations set rigid limitations on movie schedules and commercial content of movies on television. Both RAI and Reteitalia have announced that, for that reason, they will not show as many theatrical movies but will increase the number of made-for-TV movies and mini-series. So, it may be that the only way that Italian viewers will be able to see big-budget American films will be through pay-TV.

The Future

The promise of a new pay-TV market for movies and the strong coproduction business in made-for-TV movies and mini-series ensures Italy's position as a major player on the international television scene.

CHAPTER SIX

Germany

The Germans entered the last decade of the century with the dramatic destruction of the Berlin Wall and the subsequent creation of a newly united country. Although it will take many years to stabilize and resolve certain conflicts between the two former systems, the united Germany's economy is still the strongest and most dynamic in Europe. The German television business reflects the country's basic economic strength and is already well established as a major player in the global television industry. Both the state-owned networks and the private commercial channels are active coproducers with U.S. and European companies. Many more coproductions are in the planning stages. The television landscape was rounded out in the spring of 1991 with the launch of Premier, the country's first pay-TV channel, which hopes to carve out a lucrative niche over the next few years.

The Market

Germany's 25 million television homes are served by a complex combination of traditional state-owned networks and four new private channels. One public network, ARD, is composed of nine independent regional stations. The combined group has a common program schedule throughout the country. The other public network, ZDF, is managed by a combination of representatives from 11 different regions. It is a centralized business entity and, like ARD, broadcasts one schedule to the entire country.

Both public networks earn their income from consumer license fees and commercial advertising. Even though the public networks lead in the ratings, in five short years the private commercial channels have carved out a substantial audience and generate close to 40 percent of Germany's nearly $2 billion advertising market. Both of Germany's global media giants are in the private television business. The Kirch Group controls SAT-1, while Bertelsmann controls RTL Plus. Tele-5, which is partly owned by Silvio Burlusconi, targets young viewers with music-oriented programming. PRO-7 is largely a movie channel.

Cable penetration in Germany is about 40 percent and continues to grow. Nearly 60 percent of the television households have VCRs. German-produced programs are by far the most popular programs with viewers. However, German versions of The Price Is Right (Der Preis Ist Heiss), on RTL Plus, and Wheel of Fortune (Glucksrad), on SAT-1, consistently generate strong ratings for the commercial networks.

The Networks

Just as the integration of what used to be called East Germany into West Germany is a political and economic challenge, so too the integration of DEF, the former state-run East German network, into public broadcaster ARD presents complicated problems. Before the reunification, DEF had nearly 8,000 employees working in its Berlin facility. The fate of thousands of those people as well as the issue of how to integrate DEF's formerly government-controlled news media into ARD's independent approach to journalism is not yet entirely resolved. But cable companies and commercial broadcasters have no doubt about the long-term profit potential in the five German states that used to be communist East Germany. Cable has already started to wire East Berlin while SAT-1 and RTL Plus have launched major promotional campaigns aimed at attracting the millions of new viewers who have never been exposed to commercial, audience-driven, television.

Coproduction

Most experts predict that Germany's public and private networks will continue to pay increasingly competitive prices for successful American programming. As is the case throughout Europe, German program executives are aggressively pursuing coproduction opportunities with both American and other European partners. These coproductions are attractive because they allow a broadcaster to lower production costs without sacrificing production quality. Most importantly, since coproductions are creatively controlled by people from at least two countries, they have the potential to have specific market appeal as opposed to simply being imports. CapCities/ABC has been one of the most active American companies in the German market. It owns a 49 percent interest in Tele-Munchen, a Munich-based TV production and distribution company. CapCities/ABC has a sophisticated strategy for building its position in the international television market.

> We will obviously continue to try to sell that product which we produce in the States to the European market. But, I think that there is another opportunity. And, maybe even a greater opportunity for *European* production companies to market to the European market. Therefore, what we have done is to take a stake in that marketplace by buying into companies that we have known over the years, that we know to be well-managed, successful companies. We have taken

minority positions in them because we don't intend to dominate. We intend to let the local management run their businesses the way they've been running them. One dimension that we probably bring is a worldwide marketing element that could expand their horizons in terms of the number and quality of product that they are producing. In so doing we intend to participate on two levels in what we see to be the next decade's great growth areas. That is by exporting homemade products and also by producing for foreign marketplaces within those markets themselves.

> Herb Granath
> President
> CapCities/ABC Video
> Enterprises

In addition to its stake in Tele-Munchen, CapCities/ABC also has a long-term coproduction arrangement with ZDF, one of Germany's two public networks. The deal involves the creation of movies, documentaries, series, and musical programs for the international marketplace. Already in production are: a mini-series called Hotel Shanghai, a two-hour made-for-TV movie titled Interpol, and a two-part series called True Stories. All three projects are being shot originally in English and then dubbed into German. Awarding of the potentially valuable distribution rights is reflective of each partner's strengths and business interests. ZDF has the rights in German markets, ABC will handle the United States, and Tele-Munchen will distribute to the rest of the world.

The U.K. producer/distributor, Granada TV, also has formal coproduction agreements with both ZDF and NDR, one of the ARD network-affiliate stations. Both deals involve production and distribution of made-for-TV movies shot originally in English and later dubbed into German.

Media Companies

Germany's emergence as an integral part of the world television scene is largely due to the influence of its two giant media companies. Ironically, the small town of Gutersloh is the home base of

Bertlesmann, the world's biggest media company, with annual sales of about $8 billion. Bertlesmann owns companies throughout the world in the fields of publishing, broadcasting, printing, and music. Its investment in the start-up of the commercial network, RTL Plus, is about to generate significant profits. RTL Plus has become Germany's largest advertising medium. In 1990 its revenues set an all-time German record of $750 million. It is also 50 percent owner of Premier, Germany's newly launched pay-TV service. Premier offers viewers more than 400 contemporary films per year, as well as documentaries and live sports coverage. As Premier works its way to profitability over the next few years, sales experts project that it will be an on-going customer for American programs, particularly movies. Like all of Bertlesmann's other businesses, Premier is expected to become a major financial success and to contribute to the company's global media leverage.

Germany's other media giant, the Kirch Group, controls SAT-1, the commercial station with revenues in 1990 of about $310 million. Like RTL Plus, SAT-1 is also poised to turn significant profits throughout the '90s. The Kirch Group was started in the early '50s by a visionary entrepreneur named Leo Kirch. Today, the company controls European film and TV rights valued at nearly $2 billion. In addition to SAT-1, Kirch is also involved with television production and distribution, home video production, post-production, merchandising, and book clubs. Kirch was the first to see the potential of pay-TV in Germany. In 1985 he started Teleclub, a service with a program schedule based on movies whose pay-TV rights he had secured before pay-TV even existed in Germany! After witnessing the financial bloodbath experienced by Sky-TV and BSB in their competitive pay-TV start-up efforts in the United Kingdom, Kirch merged Teleclub into Germany's new Premier pay-TV service in 1991. He now shares a 25 percent stake in Premier with Bertlesmann (50 percent) and France's Canal + (25 percent). Throughout his career, Leo Kirch had made a habit of breaking new ground with his various companies. He recently experimented with a project that is surely one of the most creative approaches to solving the universal problem of channel zapping. The two big public broadcasters, ARD and ZDF, aired a Kirch-produced crime drama titled, <u>Murderous Decisions</u>, at the same time. However, one version told the story from the heroine's point of view while the other version told the story from her lover's perspective. Viewers were encouraged to switch back and forth during the program so that they could fully understand the story line. If ever a program qualified as a television event, Murderous Decisions may have set a new standard.

The Future

Although there is agreement among German market experts that the integration of East and West Germany will slow down the German economy, there is also agreement that Germany will emerge from the process with new economic vitality. The television advertising business is expected to continue to grow throughout the decade. In 1990 alone, television advertising expenditures were up 22.5 percent. Cable and pay-TV are expected to prosper. In 1991, Pro-7, one of the independent commercial broadcasters, spent over $130 million licensing American TV series. The year before, Pro-7 spent over $500 million on program acquisition. It is now spending millions to start a news operation designed to compete head-on with ARD's news programming. There is no doubt that Germany will be one of the most influential and important players in the international television marketplace of the '90s. One clue about its underlying economic strength was recently revealed with the announcement, by Time-Warner and Bertelsmann, of the creation of an all-news, CNN-type, satellite program service for the entire country.

CHAPTER SEVEN

Spain

Spain's campaign to become a player in the new global television business has been executed with lightning speed. In 1985 Spain became the last major European country to join the European common market. In 1990 the government licensed the country's first private commercial television networks. By 1991 competition for viewers between the traditional state-controlled network and the new private networks was fierce. American producers had sold hundreds of millions of dollars worth of programming to the Spanish stations, and the last great European boom market was born.

Most experts predict a healthy, expanding, Spanish marketplace in the '90s. The bulk purchasing of hundreds of hours of American programming is largely over, but Spanish broadcasters are now competing among themselves for the most desirable American product. License fees, therefore, are expected to gradually rise, and coproductions with both American and European producers should steadily increase over the decade.

The Market

Spain has about 10 million television homes. Viewership, which has traditionally averaged about three hours per day, is increasing. The television advertising market generated about $2.5 billion in 1991 and will likely increase each year by double digit numbers until the middle of the decade. Competing for those advertising dollars is an aggressive group of old and new broadcasters. The traditional public network (RTVE) has two channels that are both supported by a combination of advertising and government funding. Those two national network channels are complemented by a group of seven regional public channels, which also derive their revenues from a combination of tax generated funds and spot advertising. The new players are the three private networks: Telecinco, Antena-3, and Canal + .

With the rapid expansion of the number of television stations, Spanish viewers' tastes in programming are also changing. A Venezuelan soap opera called <u>Crystal</u> was recently the highest-rated program. Also popular are the Spanish versions of <u>Funniest Home Videos</u>, <u>Twin Peaks</u>, <u>The Price Is Right</u>, and blockbuster American feature films.

Public Networks

The two government-owned television networks, RTV-1 and RTV-2, are trying to retain their market dominance by exercising powerful leverage on two fronts. Since they can rely heavily on the government for operating funds, they are investing a fortune in original programming and outbidding their competitors for what they consider to be the most desirable imported programming. Secondly, they are using their strong ratings performance to drive up the cost of advertising. RTV-1 reportedly collects about $75,000 for its 20-second prime-time spots. Spain's local production community has been one of the prime beneficiaries of the new, aggressive program policies at RTVE. In 1991 $120 million was budgeted for the production of major television extravaganzas like Don Quixote and Requiem for Granada. American producers such as Disney, Warner Bros., MCA, and others have also benefited from multi-million dollar program purchases.

Spain's six regional networks, which were licensed during the past couple of years, are beginning to carve out a piece of the television pie. Like the national network, the regional network stations draw revenues from their respective provincial governments as well as from advertising. All six stations expect to become financially profitable before the middle of the decade. To consolidate their financial leverage they have formed a coordinating association named Forta, whose first major deal was the purchase of a package of 200 movie features from Columbia Pictures Television. Forta, on behalf of the regional government stations, paid around $100 million for the package, thus outbidding the national network, RTVE. Another regional government station, TV-3, which broadcasts in the Barcelona market, has put together a historic coproduction deal with Lorimar Television. In Barcelona, TV-3 is shooting an on-location, 22-episode dramatic series titled Dark Justice that airs late-night on CBS on Friday. The program is considered very successful by CBS, where it averages a 3.5 rating up against the Tonight Show on NBC and Nightline on ABC. Spanish industry observers anticipate the regional government channels will become even more aggressive in the international coproduction arena during the '90s.

Private Networks

The most successful of the new private commercial networks is Telecinco. Europe's most flamboyant and entrepreneurial TV executive, Silvio Burlusconi, owns 25 percent of Telecinco and exercises operational control of the network. After only six months of operation, Telecinco made history by actually beating RTVE in certain time periods! Burlusconi's program strategy includes big-budget American movies, game shows, and off-network series like Charlie's Angels and The Love Boat. Last, but not least, is a Spanish version of the popular Italian gameshow Wow, It's Hot, which occasionally features attractive hostesses who reveal total frontal nudity!

Antena 3 was the first of the new private commercial networks. It began broadcasting early in 1990. A major newspaper publisher is the controlling partner. The programming strategy is based on a combination of independent news, which is not influenced by the government, and American features and series. Locally produced dramatic programming is gradually becoming another staple for Antena 3.

The last of the new commercial networks is Canal + , which is 25 percent owned by the very successful Paris-based Canal + . Like the French pay-TV service, Canal + in Spain has built its schedule on popular American movies, documentaries, and sports. Spanish market experts are reluctant to predict success for the pay-TV network. They speculate that there are only a limited number of Spanish viewers who will pay $35 per month when there are now five channels broadcasting for free in each region. Canal + has said that it needs 300,000 paying subscribers to break even. It currently has about 150,000 and hopes to hit the magic 300,000 mark in 1993.

The Future

Spain's recent membership in the European common market, coupled with the general European economic reforms in 1992 and the Barcelona Olympics, have created a vibrant, expanding economy. The television business is riding Spain's economic wave. Predictably, the introduction of private commercial television is wreaking economic havoc on the formerly monopoly-controlled government network. A recent study reported that RTVE's two national channels only collected slightly more than 50 percent of Spain's advertising revenues in 1990. Until 1989 they controlled over 90 percent of the ad revenues. The government is expected to bail out their two financially strapped networks until the marketplace stabilizes, but there is no doubt that RTVE will eventually become a much smaller company as it adjusts to a free-market, competitive economy. Although no industry experts expect the Spanish boom to go on forever, they do predict that the importance of the Spanish market on the global television scene will continue to grow as program license fees rise and coproductions increase.

CHAPTER EIGHT

Canada

The Canadian television industry began the 1990s struggling with the twin challenges of managing its way through a serious economic recession and trying to maintain its cultural identity with Canadian-produced programming. During the '80s, Canada was able to parlay its lower production costs, its European relationships, and its proximity to the United States into an important position in the international television business. Market experts project that Canada will maintain its position in the global industry and will increase its international coproductions while decreasing its purchases of U.S.-made programs during the '90s.

The Market

Canada has nearly 10 million television homes, most of which are concentrated in the south along a 50-mile belt that parallels the U.S. border. Government funding, combined with a mature commercial advertising industry, support a large number of television stations serving both English- and French-speaking Canadians. The Canadian Broadcasting Corporation (CBC) manages the publicly funded national networks, one in English, the other in French. The private commercial national network also runs one English station (CTV) and one French service (TVA). There are also two "semi-national" private networks: Global TV, which reaches about 60 percent of the English-speaking region, and Quatre Saisons, which broadcasts to most of French-speaking Quebec.

As is the case in the United States, the networks distribute their programming through a nationwide system of affiliated local stations. There are about 80 such stations in the principal population centers of Canada. There are also about 15 independent stations that do not have a network affiliation. In addition to its extensive and complex system of television stations, Canada is also one of the most heavily cabled regions of the world. National cable penetration is over 65 percent. In some cities it reaches 85 percent! Nearly 70 percent of Canada's TV households have VCRs.

In English-speaking Canada, U.S. television programs have a tradition of popularity. In fact, Canada is the number-one international marketplace for American-made shows. *Variety* magazine estimates 1990 expenditures for American programs to have exceeded $300 million. Some Canadian dramatic productions, as well as hockey telecasts, are also very popular. But, in French Canada, locally produced programs in the French language consistently score the highest ratings numbers.

National Networks

As the '90s begin, the Canadian television industry is suffering from the effects of the worldwide economic recession and the reduction in commercial advertising expenditures. Just as the three major U.S. networks have undergone profound changes in recent years, so too have the Canadian national stations.

The CBC has two new members in top management. One was an English language producer, the second was a career civil servant, with no broadcast experience, from Quebec. The business agenda for the CBC, largely created by the government, seems to be to support an increase in the number of Canadian-produced programs. Meanwhile, at the largest private network, CTV, the new CEO is the former chief executive of Campbell's Foods, a major packaged-goods advertiser. He has caused some stir in the local industry by announcing his intention of making the network more commercially driven. Finally, after four years of internal fighting among the various owners at Global TV, Izzy Asper, a veteran broadcaster, bought out his partners and began his independent stewardship of the network. The new business strategies resulting from these dramatic management changes have not yet been entirely revealed, but experts are in agreement that the future of Canadian television will not be business as usual. It is, therefore, impossible to predict with any precision how the enormous changes impacting the Canadian television business will affect the U.S. television industry. In general, experts expect the number of independent Canadian productions and the number of international coproductions to rise. This will likely reduce the amount of programs purchased from American producers.

Coproduction

Canadian independent television producers have a long-established tradition of international coproduction with the United States, Australia, and Europe. They are well-established players in the global television game.

- My Secret Identity is a series that airs in U.S. syndication and on the CTV network. It is coproduced by Sunrise Films and MCA.

- The Nancy Drew dramatic series is coproduced by Nelvana Productions and a French production company. It airs on the U.S.A. network in the United States.

- Alliance Communications coproduces the Bordertown series as well as The Adventures of the Black Stallion

with French production companies. Both series air on
The Family Channel in the United States.

- Ray Bradbury Theater is coproduced by Atlantis Films
  and a New Zealand producer. In addition to Canada and
  New Zealand, the series is scheduled to air on the U.S.A.
  network.

The Canadian coproduction sector is thought by most experts
to have a healthy future as broadcasters continue to try to drive
down the price of programming, and as Canadian viewers become more interested in their own cultural heritage.

Local TV

Toronto is the home base for the majority of Canada's independent television producers. It is also the home of City-TV, a local
television station that many broadcasters from around the world
feel is on the cutting-edge of the future of local TV. City-TV
started nearly 20 years ago as the brainchild of Moses Znaimer,
its current president and executive producer. One of Znaimer's
guiding principles was his commitment to exploiting the experi-
ential dimension of television, both for the viewer as well as
for the station employee. City-TV is housed in a largely glass
structure which allows and encourages people to watch television
being made. There is even a sidewalk speakers corner where
anybody can record their opinions on videotape. City-TV mer-
chandise is sold in a retail store, and people are encouraged
to become audience participants in studio-based productions.
City-TV's newspeople are called videographers. To ensure that
they communicate the excitement of the news-gathering experience, they produce, photograph, write, edit, and report their
own stories. They experience the process from start to finish.
Although the City-TV approach to local news is unusual by
major-market American standards, it has resulted in a very
successful style of journalism. In the fiercely competitive Toronto market, City-TV has overtaken its rivals and is now the
number-one rated evening newscast.

Our achievement is not only that we manage a pretty good local newscast, and that we make some shows that other people will buy. It's that we've done that with a singular consistency of voice that is expressed as much in the engineering and architecture and technical infrastructure of the channel as it is in the rhetoric of the public relations department. It's the combination of those two that really marks City-TV as a potential model that can not only travel but is actually licenseable. Somebody who wants to do this sort of thing can presumably come into town and check into a hotel and if they are half professional in our business, they'll watch the station for a day or two and they'll say; I get it. I get the idea. But, the fact is that what makes it work is rigorously shot through the whole operation and intimately involved in the way we work and the place in which we work and the fact that City-TV is a pure invention, an innovation in signal distribution that is devoted to the whole notion of video verite. It's all of that that constitutes the unique and intellectual property right that people are beginning to recognize and beginning to want to emulate. Typically it's not people who are already in the business who are attracted to this model. It's people who want to get into the business, especially the players in the European theater who are confronting the same conditions of life that we did 20 years ago. City-TV had to be invented to respond to the pressure of competition at the border with the U.S.A. With the number of different signals involved, nobody needed another channel to do the same old thing. And, whoever was going to get around to it had to make it work in a economic environment which Americans can barely comprehend, except maybe small market operators. We make these shows that compete with ABC, NBC, CBS, CBC, Global TV, etc., for tiny fractions. I don't mean 20 percent less. I don't mean 50 percent less. We are competing with companies that begin at ten times and go up to a hundred or two hundred times our size. The public doesn't know this. The public can punch up ABC and right next to it is City-TV and next to that is CBC.

CBC gets a billion four hundred million dollars a year to operate. And, we beat them. That's the point.

Moses Znaimer
President & Executive Producer
City-TV

The Future

In addition to its dual role as a strong purchaser of imported programs and a major coproducer of programs within the international television marketplace, Canada may have given birth to a unique style of hyper-local programming that will be franchised during the '90s into the world's newly emerging, competitive markets.

CHAPTER NINE

Australia

The Australian television industry, once one of the hottest inter-national television markets in the world, started the 1990s in what some experts consider to be the worst economic shape in its 40 year history. It appears that it will be years before Australian television will be in a position, once again, to pay competitive prices for American programs. However, there are signs that the Australian production community will fare well in the inter-national marketplace during the '90s.

The Market

Australia has two government-funded national networks: the Australian Broadcasting Corporation (ABC), which programs general information and entertainment to the mass audience, and the Special Broadcasting Service (SBS), which programs to minorities. The public networks and their affiliates are complemented by three fiercely competitive, private, commercial networks. The Australian Television Network (formally known as the Seven Network), Nine Network, and Network Ten. These three networks compete for about $1 billion in annual advertising expenditures.

The Australian television industry has a rich tradition of well-produced local programs. The country's five million viewers prefer those home-grown shows over programs imported from Europe or the United States. The hottest domestic show is a sitcom called <u>Hey Dad</u>. The most popular U.S.-made show is <u>L.A. Law</u>.

There is no cable television in Australia. However, the government has approved licenses for several pay-TV ventures in the early '90s. About 73 percent of the television households have VCRs.

The Networks

Australia's television industry has fallen victim to the combined impact of a dramatic economic recession and the fragility of the corporate financing of its three private, commercial networks. In the mid-'80s, all three of those networks were taken over by new owners who financed their purchases largely on the basis of the stations' profit performances during the early '80s boom period. Then the recession hit. By the start of the '90s, two of the three networks, Seven and Ten, went bankrupt and were later taken over by the banks which had financed their original sales five or six years earlier. Meanwhile, the Nine Network was repurchased by its previous owner, Kerry Packer, from the debt-ridden Alan Bond for 40 percent of what Bond had paid for it a mere four years earlier.

Among other things, the corporate carnage in Australia has caused the networks to scale back their program purchases vastly, and they are only offering a fraction of the license fees for American programs that they offered during the '80s. Some networks are reportedly trying to renegotiate the terms of agreements made with American producers and distributors several years ago when the boom looked like it would last forever.

With little, if anything, to spend on new program development, the networks are now reportedly experiencing an erosion of viewers. All of this comes at a time when the advertising community is cutting back its spending in response to the impact of the general economic recession on its clients. It is, as they say, not a very pretty picture.

The Future

The bright spot on the Australian television landscape is that several Australian producers continue to do well in the international market. Reg Grundy, one of the world's most successful producers of internationally distributed programs, exports Neighbors to the United Kingdom, where it is one of the top-rated programs in the country. Grundy is also actively coproducing in France, Germany, and other European markets. Beyond International continues to export its highly successful series Beyond 2000 to markets throughout the world. It also has a number of other coproductions in various stages of development with international partners.

Although Australia will not likely be a top-dollar purchaser of American programs in the near future, market experts predict that the future for international coproductions will progressively expand during the '90s. The Australian film and television industry is also expected to work toward a stronger secondary marketplace for their movies and television programs in other parts of the world.

CHAPTER TEN

Japan

Japan's mature and prosperous broadcasting industry begins the new decade with an ambitious program to develop cable and pay-TV, as well as a controversial attempt to control the future flow of foreign television programs into the country. There are mixed signals as to the potential value of the Japanese market as a buyer of American programs.

The Market

Japan's 40 million television households are served by the famous NHK network. NHK, the world's largest public-service broadcaster, has two terrestrial network channels, one offering mass appeal programming and the other offering educational material. These networks depend on consumer license fees for their operating revenues. NHK also operates two satellite-delivered services: Channel 1, which programs news and sports; and Channel 2, which specializes in entertainment. The DBS services are financed by advertising and subscriber fees. In addition to NHK, there are five private, commercial networks: Nippon TV, the highest rated network; Tokyo Broadcasting System; Fuji TV; TV Asahi; and TV Tokyo. These private networks all have regional affiliates throughout the country.

Cable TV

Cable television has only penetrated about 20 percent of the country, mostly in rural, mountainous areas. However, most of the planned development of cable television systems in the '90s will be in the major urban population areas. Cable developers project that by the turn of the century penetration levels will be near 50 percent.

Pay-TV

Media analysts in Japan are predicting enormous growth in pay television during the '90s. They expect it to become a $2 billion business by the end of the decade. With a pot of gold of that size on the other side of the rainbow, the pay-TV wars are serious business. NHK's two services have had the field to themselves since 1988, but Japan Satellite Broadcasting (JSB), which is reportedly capitalized at over $300 million, launched a pay-TV service featuring music programs, Japanese films, and live sports on April 1, 1991. JSB also purchased DBS rights to several packages of American movies from Warner Brothers, Paramount, and Universal. The success of JSB's launch has surprised many of the market experts. Subscriber sales have been three times what was originally projected. JSB's financial break-even point is now estimated to be a mere two years away.

American versus Japanese Programming

Japan is unquestionably a major player in the international television business. Sony's ownership of Columbia and Matsushita's ownership of MCA speaks to the fact that Japan is a major contributor to the *creation* of the global television industry. But market experts disagree about whether American producers and distributors will actually profit from the Japanese television market. There are certain facts that are undeniable.

First, the simple truth is that there are very few American programs shown on Japanese television. Many Japanese programmers say that U.S. programming just does not attract an audience. Program ratings prove, however, that Japanese viewers are very interested in life outside their own country. But, both entertainment and documentary programs that are shot in foreign countries by Japanese producers, featuring Japanese actors and reporters, are by far the most popular programs.

> Japan is the single most difficult market I've ever come across. I think it will stay that way. It is a system that has been developed that is very difficult for us to work through. Their television is run by the advertising agencies. The types of programming you can put on are severely limited by their ability to *sell* to the viewers. And, their tastes seem to be not quite the same as ours. I think sports is a possibility because it requires the least amount of translation. When it comes to informational programming, they do really good stuff. So, I don't see why they would need our stuff. I don't know that they need us in the news area. And, in entertainment, it's terribly difficult to break through.
>
> Rich Frank
> President
> Walt Disney Studios

Despite Japanese viewers' clearly demonstrated appetite for locally produced television programs, half of the theatrical tickets sold to Japanese moviegoers, a total of 77 million in 1989, were for American movies.

Japan will only become a market in one area, and that's pay-TV. I don't believe that the commercial networks are ever going to program more than five or eight percent of their programming with American programs.

Michael Solomon
President
Warner Bros. International

Once again, looking just at the facts, there is no arguing with Michael Solomon. His extensive experiences in the international marketplace have prompted him to reach his conclusion. As noted earlier, he has sold a package of movies to JSB, the new pay-TV service.

Acquisitions

Just as one is tempted to reach the conclusion that there is a relatively limited potential for American programs in Japan, along comes MICO, a new company that has become the focus of a fierce controversy. Media International Corporation, known as MICO, was founded by NHK, the giant Japanese public-service network. MICO has announced that it intends to purchase Japanese rights, in all media, for programs either cofinanced by MICO or programs that are acquired outright. Japan's five commercial networks are so concerned about MICO that they released a joint press announcement publicly opposing its creation.

They said they feared that MICO's large financial and corporate backers would use MICO, and the clout of NHK, to control the software of the world in Japan. One commercial network executive was quoted as expressing concern over the creation of "a kind of 'Japan Inc.' of the mass media field" that might lead to international reactions against Japan.

While the commercial networks fear that MICO could make it very difficult for them to compete for program purchases against NHK, there is little doubt about the intent of MICO's creation. When it was announced, MICO's goals included the "accumulation in Japan of the know-how for the production of high-quality software of universal standard." MICO executive vice president, Kounosuke Suzuki, has been quoted as saying: "Japan is importing software from all over the world, and exporting nothing, and producing nothing. With the world of visual entertainment changing so rapidly, we are afraid that we won't have access to programming. It will all be controlled by someone else. If we don't create MICO, we will not be able to deal with the giants."

How the interests of the five commercial networks, who compete against NHK, will be accommodated in relationship to MICO, is yet to be resolved. But, Japanese analysts reportedly expect MICO to spend millions of dollars in the international marketplace to acquire features, major sporting events, and other television programs.

Coproduction

At the start of 1991, MICO announced a coproduction with ABC News, Gosteleradio in Russia, and NHK, to produce a one-hundred part series titled The Twentieth Century Project.

Separate and apart from MICO, NBC has announced a deal with TV Tokyo, one of the five private commercial networks. The arrangement involves distributing NBC programming in the Far East and developing coproductions with NBC. In addition, NBC News has announced a deal with Nippon Television, one of the other private networks, for exclusive U.S. rights to NTV News feeds in exchange for NTV's exclusive right to use NBC news material in Japan.

Tokyo Broadcasting has also carved out a lucrative niche in the international television business by licensing formats to its shows to broadcasters and producers in other parts of the world. TBC licensed the format to one of its most popular programs to ABC-TV. The format became the foundation of America's Funniest Home Videos, one of the top-rated programs in the United States. ABC has also licensed the format to a quiz-travel program, which it is adapting for a Saturday morning time period.

In what seems like just the latest in a never-ending series of threats to the world dominance of CNN, NHK has announced the creation of the Global News Network, a tri-polar joint venture involving itself, U.S., and European broadcasters.

The Future

The history of Japanese television is that programs have mostly been produced in Japan, by Japanese producers, for the Japanese market. Whether the emergence of pay-TV and the voracious ambitions of MICO will open the door of opportunity for American producers and distributors will be one of the most closely followed developments in the international marketplace during the '90s.

CHAPTER ELEVEN

The International Audience

Just as Marshall McLuhan predicted, in many ways the world has become a global village. The explosive development of tele-communications and computers, particularly during the last decade, has homogenized many of life's common experiences into what demographers call a "global lifestyle." People throughout the world, particularly younger people, experience the global lifestyle every day without even thinking about it. The experiences are relatively superficial. McDonald's serves hamburgers to the Japanese while Americans feast on native dishes from all the Asian cultures. For many Americans, Asian and other ethnic foods are available within minutes of home. Fashion is another barometer. The French have adopted the

Western look of denim jeans with the same gusto that American businessmen wear Italian-designed suits. Rock and roll music is heard on the sidewalks and car radios virtually everywhere in the world.

Certain types of television programming have also become elements of the global lifestyle. Throughout the world, viewers watch the same American-made movies. Live news and sports coverage is sent via satellite around the globe faster than it would take many people to discover what is going on in their own neighborhoods. Young people in hustling urban capitals and in peaceful rural villages all share the same common fashions and styles portrayed in music videos. All that is required to share in the global television experience is to be in the footprint of one of dozens of satellites transmitting programs from nearly 24,000 miles out in space.

Cultural Nationalism

While television is unquestionably on the cutting-edge of the new global lifestyle, it is also at the center of a heated international controversy. The emergence of cultural nationalism as an important social movement is directly related to the growth of the global lifestyle and to international television. While people relish and enjoy the relatively superficial opportunities offered by the new international lifestyle, they are very protective of what they consider to be their unique identity and their unique values. They think of their values and their citizenship as the truly meaningful elements that make them special members of the family of man. The refusal to be homogenized in ways that affect personal values, or that reduce the significance of local politics, is why many countries have adopted quotas to limit the amount of imported American television programs.

The emergence of English as the most popular language in the world is also partly responsible for the cultural nationalism movement. English has replaced German as the language of science. It has replaced French as the language of diplomacy. It is the first or second language for hundreds of millions of people and is the language most taught in the world's schools. Perhaps the most telling sign of the long-term importance of

English is that it is the language of the computer and communication business. In recent years social scientists have discovered that although English is becoming a universal language, it is usually supplementing, rather than replacing, native languages. This, too, is a phenomenon associated with cultural nationalism. People want to be citizens of the global village, but they also want to retain their cultural identity. As John Naisbitt has pointed out in *Megatrends 2000*, language is "the frequency on which culture is transmitted."

Global Appetites

As we approach the turn of the century, the future of international television comes into sharper focus. Because of satellite technology and the growth of private cable and DBS systems, each region of the world will move toward a television service that will allow nearly everybody to watch nearly everything. But, people will not all watch the *same* programs. Each region will offer a combination of international programs, many of which will be informational, and local programs that reflect the unique cultural qualities of the audience. Carving out a piece of the complex international marketplace, whether by producing programs that are acceptable in a variety of cultures or by coproducing programs that work equally well in several countries, is the challenge of the '90s for American program makers.

Evidence of the new international audience is everywhere. Because there has been so little communication between the United States and the U.S.S.R., Americans are fascinated with the developments in Russia. Apparently the Russians can't get enough of *Gone with the Wind*. The 50-year-old movie reportedly sold out a 2,500 seat Moscow theater during the first two months of its run. This happened despite the fact that the Moscovites had to watch the movie with a crude, voice-over narrative track. (The completion of a properly dubbed version was delayed because the studio laboratory workers were needed to help with the fall potato harvest!) Tribune Entertainment reports that Geraldo is the first American program to be given a daily program slot on Russian television. Phil Donahue and Victor Posner, the Russian talk show host, now appear in the United

States and Russia in a weekly program produced by Multimedia, which they co-host. In a development that must have older Russians scratching their heads and wondering where they went wrong, MTV has arrived in the U.S.S.R. Each Friday night MTV video-jockeys host a prime-time program that is sent out to a potential 88 million households. The Russians don't pay a license fee for the show, but MTV keeps the commercial inventory. The problems of the Soviet economy have not stopped Benetton, L.A. Gear, and Wrangler from advertising their products to what they hope will one day be millions of fashion-conscious Soviet consumers; all members in good standing of the international youth lifestyle.

Global Programming

In the United States, Intercontinental Television Group has launched a basic cable service called the International Channel. Programs featuring 15 different languages are available to about one million viewers throughout America. Even though the reverse is what has traditionally happened, some experts predict that non-U.S. produced programming will eventually influence the American creative process.

> If you walk around MIP, to the various exhibition booths, and look at the products being displayed at the non-U.S. distributors, I think you very quickly become aware that there is more of a willingness to be adventuresome in terms of subject matter, in terms of how the product is produced, in other parts of the world than there is in the United States. I think that in the United States, because of the pressures of the mass audiences needed in American television shows, we have fallen into the trap of being repetitive to the point of nauseum. Derivative has become the order of the day. I think we're beginning to see the break-out of people's willingness to accept something different and consider it. It becomes more and more acceptable. In the next decade, I see, because of expanding world communications, both East to West and West to East, I think you're going to find many

more different forms of television than you currently have in
the rather restricted U.S. market.

> Herb Granath
> President
> CapCities/ABC Video
> Enterprises

Animation

One form of programming that seems to fit well into the global
lifestyle is animation. The American and Japanese animators
have found a receptive international audience for many of their
programs for several years. Perhaps it has something to do with
the fact that younger people seem generally to be more open-
minded to foreign program concepts. Whatever the reason,
Twentieth Century Fox Television recently began selling international rights to five animated programs that were originally
produced for the Fox television network in the United States.
Many other U.S.-based distributors report strong international
interest in animated series. DIC enterprises and Silvio Burlusconi Communications have announced that they are coproducing $20 million worth of animated series during 1991. The pro-
grams will feature talent from both Europe and America.

Sports

Sports is another form of television programming that is destined
for more international exposure throughout the '90s. One sure
sign of the increased international importance of sports is the
creation of a European-based annual meeting devoted entirely
to the buying and selling of sports programming. Based at the
Lowes Hotel in Monte Carlo, the Sportel convention was
launched in the fall of 1990. More than 20 international distributors including CBS, NBC, ABC, Gosteleradio from Russia, and
Television Sport and Leisure from London offered international
rights to various televised sporting events.

Andrew Neil is currently the editor of the *Sunday Times* in
London. In 1988 and 1989 he was executive chairman of Sky
Television in the United Kingdom during its launch period. In

a speech delivered in July of 1990 in Los Angeles, he provided some insight into the role of sports on Sky TV.

> Some kinds of sport—football, tennis, golf, athletics—also cross national boundaries, so Sky has made Eurosport a genuinely Pan-European channel, using the multi-audio channels that each Astra transponder carries to broadcast the commentary in four languages. Every game in the World Cup, for example, was broadcast on Eurosport. So are many of the major golf and tennis championships. This is not a junk sports channel of car derby wrecking or dwarf-throwing; after 18 months, it's already in 20 million European homes, attracting advertisers such as Japanese automakers, who want to reach the whole European market.
>
> Andrew Neil
> Editor
> *London Sunday Times*

Eurosport is now owned by the giant French commercial network, TF-1. The potential of the international sports television market has not been lost on American producers. United Artists Entertainment and Tele-Communications Inc., the biggest cable company in America, have reportedly been planning a general sports cable program service for Europe.

The inventor of round-the-clock sports programming, ESPN, is well on its way to becoming a global program service. It debuted a Latin American service in the spring of 1991. By the end of 1991 it had a major involvement in a Japanese TV sports service as well as being a major supplier of programs to Screensport, the Pan-European sports service that is scheduled to become a 24-hour per day service.

TV News

Perhaps no other form of programming has as much potential appeal to the lifestyle of the international audience as does live television news. During the Gulf War in 1990 and 1991, America's CNN changed forever the landscape of electronic news. It was astounding to watch as the world's top political leaders communicate with each other, as well as with the people of the world, through CNN. At the beginning of the war CNN had nearly 11 million viewers in the United States alone. By the spring of 1991, CNN was reaching nearly 75 million television households in over 100 countries. No one was predicting that CNN would put any of the world's local news broadcasters out of business. If anything, CNN makes local news broadcasters more valuable to their audiences. Once viewers see the coverage of world events through CNN's electronic window, they are hungry to learn how those events relate to them directly. They depend on their local news broadcasters to bring CNN's global coverage into direct focus. Scientists and various experts will probably debate the impact of CNN on the global village until well into the next century. Some say that the audience for electronic world news was waiting for the right product. Others say that CNN created a market by producing its product and gradually proving the product's value. The truth is probably a little of each.

There has never been a successful television program that hasn't been copied. Trade journals report, from time to time, about one of the major European broadcasters, like *B-SKY-B* or the BBC, planning to launch a competitor to CNN. In December of 1990, Keiji Shima, then the chairman of NHK, Japan's giant public broadcaster, announced that he would create a competitor to CNN. He was quoted as saying, "I don't want to bad-mouth Mr. Turner, but CNN is trying to force U.S. news on the rest of the world."

Many industry observers doubt that there is room for more than one profitable global television news network. I can't help but personally remember when CNN was started back in the early '80s. I was running the news operation of the local CBS affiliate in Atlanta at the time. Since CNN was starting in Atlanta, friends from throughout the country thought that I might have some insight into the "crazy" man who was starting a 24-hour a day news operation. Most of us doubted that it would ever be possible to make such an operation profitable, but with absolute confidence we were sure that the American audience didn't want news 24-hours a day! Not only has CNN demonstrated the global audience interest in electronic news on demand, but it has prompted local news operations throughout the country to start local cable news channels. In a world where unprecedented and unpredictable events happen every day, the birth and growth of CNN has got to rank as one of the most amazing achievements in the history of television.

All three major American network news operations have announced expansions into the international television market. ABC is supplying news to Fuji TV, in Japan, among others. CBS is supplying Tokyo Broadcasting, and NBC is sending and receiving news from the Nippon Television Network. Some of this activity, however, is strictly based on financial considerations.

> We are a global village, in a news and information sense, today. I think there are a number of opportunities. A lot of them are corporate in nature because you have an enormous cost of newsgathering and an incredible amount of duplication. As networks are looking for ways to bring their costs down, I think you'll see a lot more cooperation and resource sharing which could result in actual, if not mergers of news divisions, a broad number of joint ventures. You see that now with NBC's and BBC's joint coverage of Wimbledon. You see it in a lot of newsgathering. It's one thing to put your own newsman on the ground. But, whether you need eight different guys pointing eight different cameras at eight different news reporters is a separate issue. I think there are ways to maintain the integrity of the journalistic process and save money at the same time. It's only in an era of scarce resources that people really start thinking that way.
>
> Michael Garin
> Senior Managing Director
> Furman, Selz

CHAPTER TWELVE

Cultural Nationalism and Quotas

Among the language of the principal players in the development of the global television business, there is no word and no subject that is more instantly controversial than the word quota. Most Americans, and some Europeans, see the word quota in one dimension. They interpret its purpose to be preventing them from selling their programs in countries where the viewers want to see them. Other Europeans see the word in another dimension. They intend it to mean the method by which they will prevent the Americanization of their culture. In fact, the quota controversy is much more complicated. It is where the world of European commerce and European culture intersect. It is at the heart of whatever communication gap exists between Americans and non-Americans. Understanding the quota controversy is absolutely necessary for anyone who aspires to participate in the international television business.

Government Regulation

In the non-U.S. markets, the television industry has been regulated by the government for most of its history. In some cases the government simply levied consumer license fees that were turned over to the national station and used to financially support the station's operations. In other cases, the government licensed a station to be a commercial broadcaster. In those markets, television advertising developed in a government-protected, monopolistic environment. The majority of programming was made by the stations, which depended on government protection, in one form or another, for their existence. Since there was little, if any, competition for viewers, the programming tended to reflect the interests of the station managers and government officials who controlled the system. Programming was not consumer-driven, as it has been in the United States for nearly 50 years. European viewers had very little and, sometimes, no choice, when it came to watching television. The television programs that were produced in these protected environments ran the gamut from exceptional to terrible. In some systems television became an important part of the culture of the country. Professionalism developed throughout the ranks of the production community and some of the best programs in the history of the industry were made. In other systems, television was simply an outlet for government propaganda. The production community did not develop any leverage and some of the most uninspired, amateurish television programs in the history of the medium were forced on the unfortunate viewers.

Deregulation

In the '80s, the big change occurred. Television in the non-U.S. markets began to be deregulated. Deregulation of the formerly protected television systems came about for a variety of different reasons. In some cases it resulted from the creation of satellites, which had no regard for territorial boundaries and could send programs anywhere. In some cases it resulted from consumer and advertiser pressure on governments. In yet other cases, it came about as the natural result of the growth of liberalism, an approach that values the individual's freedom of choice over government-imposed regulations. For these reasons, and others, in country after country, television has been deregulated.

Deregulation has affected television professionals, politicians, advertisers, and viewers in ways that most Americans find difficult to appreciate. Those who prospered under the protected systems feel threatened by change, and those who have benefited from deregulation, who have become part of the new systems, are insecure about how to best apply their leverage.

The European Market

While this revolutionary change was taking place in the television industry, Europeans from many different professions began the process of creating the single European market. In Brussels, home of the European Commission, Europe's equivalent to the federal bureaucracy in Washington, the politicians concluded that unless the various European countries joined together into one economic unit of 360 million consumers, they would individually be dominated by the economic powerhouses of America and Japan. To Americans, whose states realized there was strength in unity 200 years ago, the forming of the European Economic Community in 1992 seems obvious and long overdue. But, to Europeans whose countries and cultures have existed for thousands, not hundreds, of years, it is extremely threatening and very complicated.

Program Quotas

Today's raging controversy over program quotas was born in and has been debated within a larger European environment

whose citizens are simultaneously struggling with the deregulation of their television systems and the formation of a single
economy composed of many individual states. Europe is going
through a period of social change the likes of which contemporary Americans have never experienced.

At the end of 1989 the ministers of the European Community
approved the directive called "Television without Frontiers."
This directive went into effect in October of 1991 and, in its
broadest sense, allows EC television stations to broadcast without restrictions throughout the European Community countries. Among many other regulations, it also sets a common
group of standards for television advertising. What is most offen-
sive to international producers and distributors is that the directive also recommends that European television stations devote
a majority of their broadcast time to European-produced programs. The European commissioners were quick to point out
that the "Television without Frontiers" policy represented a
political commitment and not a legally binding requirement.

The question of the legality of the policy has to do with the
relationship between the courts in the various individual countries and the EC courts in Brussels. It is very complex, at best,
but the practical impact on people who want to buy and sell
television programs to any customer who wants to sell or purchase them is not difficult to understand. Most European countries either have, or are in the process of establishing, program
quotas for European-produced material. By their nature, these
quotas limit the amount of imported programming that a broadcaster can schedule. Since the huge majority of imported programming in all countries is American, the reality is that the
quotas limit the importing of U.S.-made programs. Whether
these quotas will, in fact, reduce the actual amount of
American-made programming imported into an individual European country will become clear over the next couple of years.

One of the most vocal supporters of the import quotas is Jack
Lang, the cultural minister of France. Lang has been critical
of what he perceives to be an excessive amount of imported
American programs on European television. Michael Solomon,
president of Warner Bros. International, one of the major suppliers of exported American programs, made news in 1990 when
he publicly criticized Lang, calling him "ignorant" of the televi-

sion business and denouncing the new quota restrictions. Since then, both men have lowered the public dimension of their feud. Within the ranks of the international television business, there is still serious disagreement.

> I think viewing practices will change as more of a commercial market develops because the more commercial a market is, the more mass-oriented programming you will see, and more demand for commercial programming will be there over the next ten years. The advertisers will demand it. And, the more private television there is, obviously, the advertising plays a very important role in profit and loss. I think that politicians will always try to interfere with the free-market theory, because, number one, it's politically advantageous to talk about television. It gets headlines. And, it exposes them. And, number two, they are very unhappy that they are losing control over the media, as they had before, so, they are doing everything in their power to create a controlled environment. If you took a vote today and took a vote ten years from now you would probably get a majority of the audience in favor of a free market. But, the politician today is very fearful of creating the free market. The cultural fear is strictly a front. It has absolutely no validity. If you really want to spread French culture what you do is you produce programming that is commercial enough. I do not use the word good because good is in the eyes of the beholder. I am saying commercial enough to be shown outside France. The fact of the matter is that European countries don't produce product which could, by and large, be sold and seen outside of their own country. They talk about Americans coming in and damaging their culture. But, at the same time, how many German programs do you see in Italy? How many French programs do you see in Spain? Very, very few and far between.

Michael Solomon
President
Warner Bros. International

One school of thought on the quota issue is that for practical purposes it is a non-issue because the expansion of television stations throughout Europe has created such a large need for programming that local Europeans could not possibly produce all that was needed. Jean Dondelinger, the EC commissioner for media and one of the architects of the "Television without Frontiers" directive, wants to put the quota issue to rest.

To pose the problem of relations between Europe and its partners in terms of protectionism or cooperation is to pose a false problem. Let's examine the European market facts. Due to liberalization in this sector, in which the directive "Television without Frontiers" is a key element, the total broadcasting time is going to rise from 260,000 hours in 1987 to 400,000 hours in 1995. A recent study estimated the European program segment of this market, as defined in the directive, at 68 percent in 1988. It can thus be deduced that the growth of the market is going to benefit both European and non-European producers, especially Americans. What does the directive envisage in Article 4, which sets the so-called quotas? 'The member states will ensure at every possible opportunity and by the appropriate means, that broadcasting organs reserve for European works a major part of their broadcasting time to the exclusion of time reserved for information, sports, and gameshows, advertising or telex.' But, what about fiction programs, designed to be broadcast at peak viewing times? In 1989 they comprised 18,500 production hours, a figure which should rise approximately 50 percent in five years. European fiction comprises 2,000 hours, i.e., 11 percent of its own market. European production is thus not in line with European market demand. The situation of European production on the world market is even worse. European products in the United States and Japan are less than 2 percent of audiovisual and cinema programming. A final observation: the European market is partitioned. Eighty percent of European productions never leave their native land.

Jean Dondelinger
EC Commissioner for Media

Despite Dondelinger's case for the practical irrelevance of quotas, I listened to speaker after speaker address the quota issue

at the first European Media Summit, held in Luxembourg in
1990.

> I'd like to open with a statement by Dr. Gyorgy Suranyi, state
> secretary for the national planning office in Hungary. During a
> talk on the 21st of September in 1989 in Budapest, he said:
> "Isn't it strange that we [Hungarians] are deregulating and
> liberalizing, while the EEC is reregulating and increasing
> legislative control?" I loved the pragmatism and lucidity of this
> statement. Since then I've been trying to find the underlying
> reasons why we Europeans have the obsession of trying to
> reregulate everything. Is it our heavy European bureaucracy? Is
> it the overpowering will to compromise by over-legislation in so
> many areas of little importance since we can't seem to agree on
> the big issues? Or, is it because we Europeans have so few
> essential problems that our politicians are blowing every minor
> issue out of proportion? I honestly haven't found the answer
> yet. But I expect it all is linked to the changes over the last 30
> years in our political, social, and economic environment and
> that the power has slipped out of the hands of the politicians,
> media, and manufacturers into the hands of the consumer. The
> consumer never had it so good because he has the power to
> choose or not to choose—not to choose a politician or a party,
> not to choose to watch a specific TV channel, not to choose this
> or that store, or not to choose this or that spaghetti brand. The
> consumer goods manufacturers have come to realize the shift of
> this power over the last ten years and many are changing their
> marketing philosophies to survive in the future. Today, any
> manufacturer without strong brands and without a strong
> corporate identity is doomed. The same with political parties,
> politicians, supermarkets, and media if they let themselves
> become commodities or just conduits.
>
> Michel Reinarz
> Director of Visual
> Communications
> Nestlé Co.

That day in Luxembourg the speeches were delivered with
passion. Some speakers were combative. Some, like Reinarz,

came at the problem from a direction other than the broadcasting point of view. And, some walked a thin diplomatic line.

> The BBC's job is to serve our viewers and listeners with the best, most varied programming we can lay our hands on. We wish to be free to choose that programming from wherever we believe the best programs are available; to find the best, to produce or acquire it, and to broadcast it. Good programs arise from the variety of experience. And, in that, Europe is particularly rich. It is also our job to safeguard our access to the best and to preserve and sustain the systems which make such diversity possible. Although for us that means the rejection of quotas, it also means active involvement in discussions about the way our industry should progress.
>
> Michael Checkland
> Director General
> BBC

Some speakers were willing to look into their crystal balls and make predictions about the future of international television in general, and European television specifically.

> The European Community has a dual purpose. It desperately wants to build European film and television production industries to rival those of America by developing a highly fragmented set of national industries worth $25 billion in 1990 into a European television industry, without frontiers, worth $35 billion by 2000. Then there is the cultural argument. Film and television are the best means of breaking down barriers and building the identity Europe still lacks. The audio-visual industries reflect the cultural diversity that is Europe. Europe's strength is its cultural diversity. Its weakness is the fragmented production and distribution economics that result from that diversity. I doubt that we will solve the financing of European television programs until we resolve that conflict. European deregulation is creating a host of new channels, all hungry for programming. Demand considerably outstrips supply. Opportunities are certainly growing, but the single market, as it applies to television

programs, is likely to remain a bureaucrat's dream for a very long time to come. The viewing habits and tastes of French farmers and German grocers, of British bakers and Belgian bankers, are not about to change overnight in 1993. We will, I am sure, continue to see strong national networks producing domestic programming in their own languages for the foreseeable future. European coproductions of drama and entertainment will grow in volume but only slowly. This will be true until and unless we develop a European culture. Like most British people, I am committed to Europe. But, its cultural identity will prove to be the sum of its separate cultural identities, rather than the melting-pot that created the American culture.

Richard Dunn
Chairman of the ITV Association
CEO of Thames Television PLC

The Debate

The quota issue is a serious and emotional subject within the ranks of the international television business. After two days of listening to a truly distinguished parade of European leaders address the issue, I must say that I came away with mixed feelings. First, I came away with a new sensitivity for the attitudes that many Europeans have about American programs. They feel that American exports, everything from hamburgers to jeans, to rock and roll, to hotels, to movies and television programs, are overtaking and corrupting their native cultures. At the end of 1990, *Variety* magazine reported a speech by a Canadian television executive to a group of Hollywood executives. He reportedly rebuked the U.S. film and television community for its "archaically arrogant American approach" to European coproduction. "This new Europe," he said "is resentful of its traditional role as the dumping ground for U.S. programs. Europeans, led by the French, are increasingly protective of their market. A plethora of subsidies and quotas are being continually expanded to ensure that European producers and broadcasters retain the lion's share of their market for indigenous product and coproductions in which they play an active role.'' It is clear that future European coproductions will have to be partnerships in more than name only.

I also came away from the Luxembourg meeting thinking that it would take a long time, probably well beyond the turn of the century, to develop a true, European-based production industry that will rival and compete with the U.S. industry. For example, I imagine it will be just as difficult for a Spanish producer to make a commercially successful local program that also succeeds in, say, Germany, as it will be for that same producer to make a locally successful program that is also popular in the United States.

Finally, I came away with a sense that although the European television industry has been deregulated, many politicians, particularly, did not fully realize the power of the commercial forces that they had released into the marketplace. I expect that as television becomes more consumer-driven, and as the power and social influence of television advertising develops, it will become just as difficult for any single element of the society to control the source of programming in Europe as it would be in the United States.

Rupert Murdoch is the founder of one of the world's most overtly aggressive global media companies. He has spent a career maneuvering around various government media restrictions on several different continents. When I spoke to him at the end of 1990, he did not seem overly concerned about the current debate in Europe.

> Yes, they [Europeans] are going to limit the amount of
> American programs. But, you know, Hollywood is the
> international capital of the television industry. They make
> programs for the whole world. So, you will see a lot of
> relationships between companies in various parts of the world
> to produce global programs in Hollywood.
>
>   Rupert Murdoch
>   Chairman
>   News Corp.

Larry Lammatina is the president of EC Television Inc., a division of the global media giant, Interpublic. He has developed what may well be the most ambitious and honest European coproduction of all time. Riviera, a pre-sold, 260-episode soap opera, premiered throughout Europe in the fall of 1991. I asked Lammatina about the feelings that some Americans have that the quotas are a way of creating a "fortress Europe" for American programs.

> I don't see a fortress Europe. I don't see that at all. I see European stations wide open for good ideas wherever they come from. But, they are tired of having the American point of view run the project. When there is a large investment from an American broadcaster or producer, that broadcaster or producer feels entitled to give more input than I think some of our European friends would like. They are looking for more balance.
>
>   Larry Lammatina
>   President
>   EC TV

The debate over cultural nationalism and quotas also has to do with the simple matter of national pride. It is a matter of constant frustration to most European producers that Americans seem so insistent on placing their programs on various European stations while, at the same time, American broadcasters are so reluctant to air anything from outside the United States. Is it because European television is just not good enough to attract American viewers? Or, is it because Americans are just as provincial as anybody else?

> Up to now, there have been damn few programs that have been produced outside the United States that have found their way on to American networks. And, I think that will continue to be a very slow process, just based on the way that the networks develop their products and the pressures on the networks to deliver the large mass audiences. It's not true on the cable-originated networks. There is far more tolerance there because their thrust is not aimed at the mass audience but at very specific audiences. Within that specific arena you will find a great range of tastes. For instance, we have an ownership

position in the Arts and Entertainment network. We were one of the first when we started the Arts and Entertainment network. Because of program availability and costs, we came to Europe where state-run networks had produced culturally oriented programming for many years which found very little market in the United States and therefore had little value. So, we got it inexpensively. That was the backbone of the original programming schedule of A&E. We negotiated early on a long-term coproduction deal with the BBC because we needed quality dramas and the BBC is one of the best at producing quality dramas. There has been, therefore, a demonstrable market for European product in American cable and we think it will continue. The problem in international coproduction is that those who have been involved, for whatever reason, continue to hope that they will find a home for that production on one of the American over-the-air networks. Very often they have overestimated what the American contribution in dollars would be to their production budget. This led to a disappointment on many fronts and a rap against international coproduction and their ability to make it in the United States.

> Herb Granath
> President
> CapCities/ABC Video
> Enterprises

The history of international coproduction is filled with tales of broken promises, misunderstandings, misrepresentations, and creative frustration. Despite these experiences, the undeniable reality is that as competition increases in all the television markets of the world, and as various stations fight for smaller pieces of the financial pie, international coproductions will increase. This will be the case because most stations and networks will simply not be able to afford to make big-budget programs on their own. They will have to defray the costs with a production partner. This growing openness may also reduce the need for quotas.

> I think it's a question of timing and giving them [the Europeans] the opportunity. If you take the United Kingdom, there's been a restriction here as long as I can

remember; a voluntary restriction on the amount of imported programming, particularly American programming, that the ITV companies were allowed to show. It's a perfectly reasonable restriction. It has allowed the British broadcasters to build up their own skills and their own programs, while still allowing them to import a certain amount of American material. I think it's just a question of balance, really.

Brian Jacobs
Co-Chairman
Leo Burnett Limited, London

The debate over program quotas will be a source of on-going controversy in the international television business throughout the 1990s. Ultimately, when you whittle it down to its essence, it is about hundreds of millions of dollars in business, and it is about cultural pride. Quotas are the result of the intersection of those two issues. As the global television industry really takes shape during the last decade of the twentieth century, we are learning with an appreciation for the irony that, as the world becomes an electronic village, the world's people cling even more strongly to their native cultural identity.

You will hear, during the course of this media summit [the first media summit in Luxembourg], which is very important, all about quotas. I absolutely agree with quotas. However, I would like them to change that word. Spell that word quota a little differently. They should spell it Q–U–A–L–I–T–Y. Quality should be the only quota; not where the programs come from.

Lord Lew Grade
Chairman and CEO
The Grade Company, London

That comment by Lord Grade, delivered during a luncheon at the European Media Summit, was probably the only public statement on the quota issue during the two-day meeting that generated a standing ovation from all the participants.

CHAPTER THIRTEEN

Financial Consolidation: Europe

By the turn of the century, the European Community will be the world's largest financial market. There will be a central bank, called the Eurofed, modeled after the Federal Reserve Board in the United States. There will be a single, supercurrency competing against the dollar for global financial importance. That, in any case, is the goal of the 12-member European Community. The process of creating an EC superpower formally begins in 1992.

Europeans have tried many times over the years, with varying degrees of success, to join their efforts together for common goals. But, the 12 countries that make up the European Community are not the same as the 50 states that make up the United States. It is much more difficult than that. There are tremendous differences in culture, language, and commerce that separate the EC member countries. This has always been the case. Italy, for example, is as different, in many ways, from Finland as it is from America. However, never before have the social and economic forces of nature been as compelling for a union of European countries as they are at the start of the '90s. It is clear to even the most independent-thinking Europeans that some degree of economic and social unity is necessary if Europe is going to share global power and influence with the United States and Japan in the 21st century.

Television in the EC

Within that overall context, the leaders of the European television industry and the politicians and bureaucrats, who are administering the creation of the new European Community in Brussels, have been debating the future of television in Europe.

> Let me stray for a moment into the wider policy area of how best to stimulate European production. The debate got off to a bad start with an over-emphasis on excluding foreign material. I am glad to see increasing evidence of European initiatives to encourage coproductions and to stimulate the audio-visual industry. We need to bolster these moves to increase production by ensuring that the re-use of good quality European productions is not hampered by restrictive practices. It is possible to buy much American product at marginal prices, in part, because the American market itself, through size and through its well-developed secondary markets, gives a secure financial home base. Europe needs to develop a secondary market too.
>
> Anthony Simonds-Gooding
> Former Chairman
> BSB

The "well developed secondary markets" Simonds-Gooding is referring to in the United States include station syndication, cable, and home video. Logical and rational as Simonds-

Gooding's position is, many European experts have serious doubts about the practicality of a secondary marketplace for European-produced programs within the EC.

It is quite amazing to consider that the concept of Europe 1992 for a large part has been prompted by modern communication technology. Suddenly national governments found they were losing their monopolies in communication to their national audiences. Satellites don't care much about terrestrial boundaries. Satellites therefore became a political issue. This is combined with an increasingly powerful *individual* who both as a *voter*, and as a *consumer*, has made the process irreversible. Just think of the tremendous reversal process that is taking place in Eastern Europe. Today, governments, media, and industry are virtually powerless against the strength of the people. And, this consumer we'd better not forget. So the politicians, media, and manufacturers had better be really nice to the consumer because, he might not choose them! In this context, I want to make a few points about electronic media developments in the new Europe. The more harmonization and the more one talks of the "United States of Europe," the more Europeans will increase their chauvinism and make themselves different from other Europeans. Regional identities within national boundaries will also increase as a counterbalance. But, at the same time, the Euro-consumer will profit from each benefit he can obtain from being a European citizen. Most Europeans are learning English as a second language in school. But, please beware of the mistake that English is therefore going to be, in 10 or 20 years, the universal European language. The same emotional forces as the individual roots will force the entrenchment and defense of the national languages. The latest example is the revival of the Cornish language with raging arguments between the 180 persons who speak this old Celtic language.

> Michel Reinarz
> Director of Visual
>   Communications
> Nestlé Co.

Media 92

Many studies have been commissioned in recent years to analyze the future of the European television scene. Some of the actual numbers are different, but the trends and conclusions are nearly all the same. The European countries combined buy more than $1 billion worth of American programming each year. As more stations and networks sign-on in Europe, this number will grow throughout the decade. The output of home-grown programming is not nearly sufficient to meet the demand for prime-time drama programming, which is most popular with the viewers in each country. Of the programs produced in a particular country for that country's audience, 90 percent are never shown anywhere else except that country. Since European television is becoming privatized, more and more competitors are fighting for the limited revenue sources in each country and region. As profits are squeezed and expenses have to be contained, stations face the prospect of not being able to afford to make the expensive local dramatic programs that their audiences like. To stimulate the trafficking of television programs between countries, the European Commission created a program called Media 92.

> The principal action lines [of Media 92] are the following: The creation of an environment favorable to production, multilingualism in TV-programs, the setting up and improvement of financial mechanisms. The objective is to improve the circulation of European works on the one hand, and, on the other, to establish conditions which will allow European producers to offer competitive products in terms of both quality and price. The program also possesses a prospective dimension regarding new audio-visual services, development of audio-visual activities in regions where the means for these are lacking, and collaboration with professionals from non-Community countries, especially those of Eastern Europe.
>
> Jean Dondelinger
> EC Commissioner for Media

In the waning hours of 1990, the European parliament approved a $250 million funding package, over five years, for the

Media 92 program. There are actually 12 separate projects all grouped under the Media 92 banner. Several of those projects give some insight into the television activities which the politicians and bureaucrats will be supporting through 1996.

- BABEL, Broadcasting Across the Barriers of European Language, promotes multilingualism. Its purpose is to financially support dubbing and subtitling, as well as training programs. More than 60 TV programs from more than 20 countries have reportedly been dubbed or subtitled for broadcasting on various European television stations.

- EURO-AIM, European Organization for an Independent Audio-Visual Market, offers marketing and promotion services for independent European television producers. The EURO-AIM booths can be seen at the major European television markets, including MIP and MIP-COM. EURO-AIM was one of the first experimental programs of the Media 92 project. It has reportedly participated in the launching of nearly 400 European coproductions since it began in 1988.

- Script, also known as the European Script Fund, stands for Support for Creative Independent Production Talent. The Script fund is one of the highest profile Media 92 projects. It is chaired by Sir Richard Attenborough and gives loans for the writing of screenplays and for preproduction costs of film and television fiction. Media 92 reports that thus far, more than 60 scripts have been written. Three of those have been made into films and another dozen are in various stages of serious development.

- EAVE, the European Audiovisual Entrepreneurs, offers educational opportunities in the financial, managerial, and legal areas of European production for beginning producers.

- MBS-Media, a business school for program professionals, organizes seminars on current topics and trends in the European television business.

The supporters and administrators of Media 92 are careful to point out that their efforts are not anti-American. The goal, they say, is to help create a single European market for television programs. Although many international television executives support the objectives of Media 92 in theory, there is considerable doubt about the long-term impact of the Brussels-based project.

Governments, and the European Community, have a role to play in stimulating a more European approach. But, I think the most useful thing they can do is to interfere less, not more. We need regulation, but, as much as possible, it should come from broadcasting and regulatory professionals, not from distant legislators. Money for programs will be tighter as competition bites on established sources of funds. We will need partnerships within Europe, but we should not build a fortress Europe in an effort to exclude Americans, Australians, or other valuable coproduction partners. Meanwhile, we must do everything to maximize advertising income: more minutes perhaps, or more Pan-European advertising campaigns sold to more national broadcasters, thus enabling them to harden their softening rates. We must build the subscription markets, pioneered by Canal Plus and now being promoted by BSB and Sky. (The two merged at the end of 1990.) When successful, subscription television will bring a valuable additional source of finance for television production. We must develop secondary European markets as soon as possible to profit from the recycling of our libraries, another valuable source of new program finance, and we must push ahead with new forms of program finance like sponsorship and bartering. Judging by the level of enthusiasm and determination I see in the eyes of my own producers and production executives, I believe that the business is in good hands and that with increasing opportunities for the professionals to meet and swap projects they will find ever more ingenious ways to meet the program requirements of our viewers at home, in the European Community, and worldwide.

Richard Dunn
CEO
Thames Television

Eastern Europe

The efforts to politically consolidate some of Western Europe's financial clout in the television industry is happening at a time of unprecedented, revolutionary change in Eastern Europe. The promise of an essentially untapped marketplace of 500 million potential viewers appears, at first blush, to be an international distributor's dream come true. But, since democracy movements began in full force in 1989, projections have been tempered by the slow, painful emergence of new republics. Industry experts generally concur that the East European markets will open, one by one, as they develop convertible currency and political independence, but it will be a slow process that will evolve well into the next century.

Among the first indications of a developing East European market is the joint venture announced by Time–Warner and United International Holdings to operate the cable system in Hungary. No dollar value was announced. Time–Warner will manage the development of program services including news, sports, and entertainment, while United International will oversee the hardware side of the business. Caution and patience are the bywords for projecting the emergence of the East European markets.

> The impatience for change that you've seen in Eastern
> Europe, to a large extent fed by television, probably most
> significantly in East Germany; the pace of that change, from
> the collapse of the Communist empire, and the anticipation
> of those people to embrace the free-market philosophy of the
> rest of the world and to see, somewhat superficially, what
> they think could be a new freedom for them, is leading, I
> think, to immense problems in Eastern Europe. Because all
> of those people, if they are going to move to the more
> democratic free-market systems like the rest of the world, are
> going to have to face many problems; economic problems,
> problems between East and West Germany, unemployment,
> and the movement of people.
>
> David Plowright
> Chairman
> Granada Television

The wisdom of developing the financial potential of a country or region has also spread as far east as Russia. Late in 1990, the nearly 120 million Soviet TV-viewers who watch weekend news programs on the government network, have also seen their first Western-style TV commercials. Gosteleradio, the government network, has recently restructured its four stations and will allow 20 percent of the airtime of those stations to be commercials.

Although Soviet citizens in general have little, if any, disposable income, the ad agency that placed the spots in the weekend news thinks now is the time to begin establishing brand names. Publieuropa, an agency that is controlled by Silvio Burlusconi, placed ads for Rochas perfume, Bennetton watches, and Brooklyn chewing gum in anticipation that, one day, the Soviet Union will be a consumer marketplace.

Satellite Delivery

As Europeans attempt to better consolidate their program-making efforts in television and in politics, a consolidation in the satellite delivery business is also underway. The phenomenal success of the Astra satellite was outlined by Andrew Neil, the editor of the *London Sunday Times*, during a 1990 speech in California.

> The most interesting changes are taking place at the Pan-European level, because satellites have made it possible to broadcast to all of Europe at once. That's for one major reason, and it's called Astra. Astra is a medium-powered satellite system launched from French Guiana by the European Arianne rocket in December 1988, with a 16-channel capacity and a footprint big enough to cover most of Europe from Portugal to Greece, including much of Eastern Europe. It supplies cable systems across the continent; but, it is also powerful enough to be received direct to home (DTH) on 45cm. to 60cm. satellite dishes. The Astra story is a triumph both of freedom of expression and of private initiative in a broadcasting environment traditionally dominated by national broadcasting monopolies.

At a time when the values of freedom and market economy are reshaping the map of Europe, Astra, in its own way, has been a great example of that new freedom, beaming new channels across the continent. At present all Astra's 16 transponders are already in full use. Four are used by the Sky television network I played a part in launching in February 1989; Sky News, Sky Movies, Sky One, and Eurosport. There is a second sports channel, Screensport, owned by a British retailer, which also transmits a lifestyle channel. There is European MTV, five German channels, two Dutch, and two Scandinavian. Astra is already in more than 20 million homes via cable and DTH.

Andrew Neil
Editor
London Sunday Times

By the beginning of 1991, Astra's emerging importance on the European satellite scene was made even clearer when it launched its second satellite. Its owners confidently predicted that all 16 transponders would shortly be occupied with programming and that a third Astra satellite would be launched in 1993, followed by a fourth in 1994. Dr. Pierre Meyrat, director general of Societe Europeenne des Satellites, told the extraordinary story of Astra's success to the international audience attending the media summit in Luxembourg in 1990.

It was almost unthinkable, five to ten years ago, that a private company could operate a television satellite in Europe. The control of telecommunications and television distribution by governments and by their international satellite operating organizations, seemed to many to be an insurmountable obstacle. In many cases the satellite broadcaster was unable to uplink from the country of origin. It was illegal in many countries to own a satellite television reception dish. Astra's potential clients faced at the time equally difficult obstacles such as national control of cable redistribution, national control of program and advertising content, and protection of the existing national broadcasters. But, it would appear that market demand and business sense have overcome these obstacles. It is the consumer who triggers progress and deregulation. It was this spirit of commercial "free-thinking" that led Societe Europeenne des Satellites to conceive in 1985, in response to client demand, a television satellite which met four essential criteria: the reception equipment must be simple and cheap enough to be accessible to a mass market; the coverage area of the satellite must be big enough to reach all the homes targeted by each programmer, whether it is the British Isles, German-speaking countries, the Scandinavian, the Benelux or other markets. The choice of programs must be wide and attractive enough to trigger the installation of reception antennas by viewers, and the programs must be of a quality sufficient to sustain viewer satisfaction and therefore continued antenna market growth.

> Dr. Pierre Meyrat
> Director General
> SES

In certain European countries, satellite-to-home distribution seems to have a giant lead over cable delivery systems. In other countries, like the United Kingdom and France, cable is still being actively developed.

The generality that can be predicted is that DBS, which has not to this point been a factor in the United States, will get far more attention in the non-U.S. markets than it did in the United States. The reason that it will, I think, is that because economically it would appear to be a less expensive form of distribution for the provider. Running cables through streets is a very expensive process. The reason that cable gained the upper hand in the American market is because of the head start they had. Many people forget that cable has been in the United States for 25 or 30 years. In the early going it was primarily utilized to get the product to areas that could not pick up over the air signals. And the CATV business was really the beginning of what is now the cable industry. That does not exist in Europe or in the Pacific Rim to the extent that it did in the United States. Therefore, starting fresh, I think many of the countries will opt for some form of a DBS distribution. But, I don't think that's for certain yet. Looking at the United Kingdom, which has had a little more experience than some of the other European markets, cable has been like a punch-drunk fighter. It's been up. It's been down. Much of that had to do with the attitude of the government, encouraging or discouraging investment in cable, and they have done several flip-flops under Margaret Thatcher. So, you never discount the role of federal regulation in what will emerge as the primary distribution system.

> Herb Granath
> President
> CapCities/ABC Video Enterprises

Pan-European Programming

Various efforts to financially consolidate Pan-European programming efforts are well underway. Five major European broadcasters are pooling their efforts to produce a weekly European news magazine called Extra. Each of the five partners will produce its own local segment and then receive the remaining program elements from the other four members. The founding members of the program cooperative include BBC-2, RAI-2 (Italy), SVT (Sweden), TVE (Spain), Antenne 2, and FR-3 (France).

Once native language tracks are cut for each of the non-local segments, the programs air in similar time periods on the same night throughout Europe. The pilot for the series, which debuted in August 1990, featured a thematic program on the always popular topic of sex. The topics covered included: reverse sex discrimination in Sweden, transvestites in Naples, the secret bordellos in Birmingham, pornography in Hungary, and problems faced by Muslim women in Paris.

Ambitious as the Extra magazine project is, the more difficult challenge for Pan-European coproduction seems to be in the area of fiction programming.

> Is there a funding gap in providing for Europe's prime-time fiction requirements, and, if so, can it be financed? Let's

analyze supply and demand. The television industry in the United States in 1990 will generate roughly $500 of income per household, 60 percent of which is advertising and 40 percent subscription fees. In Europe, the industry currently generates about $183 per household, split about 50/50 between advertising and license fees. The United States spends roughly $6 billion per year on prime-time quality TV fiction, or roughly $67 per household. Comparable program cost statistics are difficult to find for Western Europe. We know U.S. exporters will sell about $1.4 billion worth of programs to Western Europe in 1990, almost all of it for prime-time fiction. In total, we estimate a further $2.5 billion per annum will be spent within Europe for prime-time fiction. That's $32 per household total, of which $12 will go to the United States; $20 only is spent in Europe—or about 1/3 of what the United States spends per household. Europe, with at least 40 percent more TV households than the United States, spends less than half as much per year within its own borders on prime-time fiction.

Patrick Cox
NBC Europe

Perhaps the most ambitious prime-time, Pan-European program effort to date is Riviera, a $40 million series being filmed in France. The huge project has been put together by EC TV, a unit of Interpublic Group of companies, the global media enterprise. Riviera's story line involves the lifestyles and power plays of an old-line European family whose commercial interests are now in the international perfume business. A total of 260 episodes are being produced at an average cost of $150,000 each. The five broadcasters who bought the show before it went into production were able to have creative input into the development of characters who represent their own nationality. These networks include, TF-1 in France, Rete-4 in Italy, Studio Hamburg in Germany, Granada TV in England, and the regional Forta stations in Spain.

When you add together the big five European countries: Britain, France, Italy, Germany, and Spain, there are

enough TV-homes and sufficient advertising revenue that
those five countries can make anything they want. What has
not occurred yet on any continuing on-going basis is a
consortium of those five countries. The way we were able to
do our soap opera was that we have commitments from those
five countries for the program; it's the first series that's ever
been done on that basis. There have been a lot of one-shot
made-fors and mini-series, but no on-going series like
Riviera, which is 260 half-hours. But, once you get those five
countries in the boat creatively, financially, they are of a size
that they can compete with anyone. Everyone understands
that. But, it hasn't been done before. It takes a long time.
It's taken us two years to put that deal together. Patience is
not a virtue of a lot of folks living in Hollywood. They like to
have a meeting to talk about it, maybe have one or two other
meetings, and do a deal. It just doesn't happen that way.

> Larry Lammatina
> President
> EC TV

The fact that Riviera ever got off the ground defies the odds
in the international programming business. The fact that the
cost of production will be entirely covered without a sale in the
U.S. market is a preview of the future importance of Pan-
European coproductions.

As is evidenced by the growing worldwide popularity of CNN,
informational programming is one form of television that travels
well through different cultures. No good television idea lasts
very long without competition, and CNN is no exception. A
group of major European broadcasters including RAI in Italy;
ARD and ZDF in Germany; TF-1, Antenne 2, and FR-3 in
France; and TVE in Spain, have announced a $10 million proj-
ect to launch a 24-hour news channel in Europe. The service is
scheduled to be operational in 1992 and will be delivered by
satellite in a variety of European languages. The all-news channel is still in the planning stages, but each member station will
reportedly contribute stories to the service and will share in the
operating costs. The founders plan to apply to the Media 92
program at EC headquarters in Brussels for additional funding.

The American Market

The financial clout of Europe's emerging television industry is already being felt in the traditionally closed American market.

In December of 1990, two first-run programs were credited with being kept in production because of their international value. Freemantle International guaranteed advance overseas sales of $400,000 per episode to LBS Communications for the former NBC series Baywatch. Although it is no longer on NBC, Baywatch will go into domestic syndication in the United States and international distribution in Europe. Steven Cannell is producing a first-run, hour-long series called Street Justice. He has reportedly credited the economic potential of the European market as being a significant part of the reason why he is launching the action-adventure series.

CBS has commenced what has been called the most ambitious experiment in international coproduction ever attempted by a U.S. broadcast network. The network has ordered a total of 110 hours of internationally coproduced action-drama hours for its latenight schedule. Those involving European coproducers include:

- Scene of the Crime, a Steven Cannell production being shot in Vancouver and Paris.

- Dark Justice, a Lorimar production being staged in Barcelona.

- Fly by Night, produced by Canada's Alliance Communications and Steven Denure in Vancouver and Nice, France.

Just as there are more programming failures than successes in the American business, no one expects all the Pan-European efforts to consolidate their financial resources to be hits. However, the consolidation of the financial clout of Europe's aggressive broadcasters is a trend that will develop rapidly throughout the '90s.

CHAPTER FOURTEEN

Financial Consolidation: Global

The financial consolidation of the programming business, involving some of the world's best known corporate giants, was the highest profile media trend at the start of the '90s. Much of the coverage of the consolidation trend involves the superficial "Japan takes over Hollywood"-type stories. More thoughtful pieces analyze the logic and reasoning behind the trend and question everything from the control of program content to the issue of whether bigger really is better. Despite the exploitation of the story in the industry press, there is no question that the stakes are enormous in the global programming business.

Programming

A study released by the New York and London-based research firm of Frost and Sullivan predicts that the international market for television programs will grow from about $2.8 billion in 1990 to about $5 billion in 1995. The U.S. share of this business is expected to be about $3 billion. This tremendous growth is happening at a time when America's economic power in many industries is being undercut throughout the world. The global distribution of American-made television programs and movies is so strong and pervasive that it constitutes the country's second largest export and is a major component of America's financial balance of trade.

The global power of Hollywood all stems from the fact that American-made television and movies seem to be an almost uniquely American product that is nearly universally acceptable. So far at least, neither the Europeans nor the Japanese have been able to duplicate them. Since the private, commercial television business is expanding in all the corners of the earth, and since U.S.-productions will supply the major percentage of the new demand, many non-U.S. companies figure that owning a piece of Hollywood is the best way to participate in the boom. The trend toward financial consolidation shows no signs of letting up.

> The driving forces affecting the television programming business basically start with a consolidation that's been going on for the last couple of years in the industry. That consolidation is brought about by a number of factors; not the least of which is, if not a drying up of, certainly less access to the capital markets. So, entrepreneurial companies which were the focus of the industry in the '80s find it very difficult to exist and compete today because they don't have the capital access to really build and expand their operations. That's an important factor. But, that really serves as a catalyst to trigger what has now become a major consolidation of the industry where I'd say for the next decade the competitive factors are going to principally be factors of scale.
>
> The smaller companies are finding it very difficult to

compete because the price of everything has gone up. The risks have essentially become a game for big companies.

> Michael Garin
> Senior Managing Director
> Furman, Selz

Finances

The capital that has fueled the financial consolidation of the entertainment business has largely flowed into the United States from non-U.S. companies. Five of Hollywood's major studios had changed ownership by the beginning of the '90s. Four of the seven (Fox, Columbia, Universal, and MGM) are now owned by non-U.S. corporations.

The largest deal of all was the $6.6 billion acquisition of MCA, the owner of Universal, by Japan's Matsushita Electric Industrial Company. MCA, the owner of *Jaws, E.T.,* and Miami Vice, says the acquisition gives it the financial leverage to continue to expand in the global entertainment industry. Matsushita is betting that it will benefit from the synergy of being in both the electronic hardware and software businesses. Before it purchased MCA, Matsushita was the 12th largest industrial company in the world. Best known in the United States for its consumer electronics products marketed under the Technics, Quasar, and Panasonic labels, Matsushita controls an empire of 87 Japanese companies and nearly that many outside the country. Its estimated 1990 revenues were $45 billion.

> MCA's position has been tremendously enhanced. I could go through all the things you read in the trade magazines about bigness; Time-Warner, Sony-Columbia. It has vaulted us into the top rungs of the ladder from, let's say, the middle rungs of the ladder in terms of our financial strength. It's peculiar. This is nothing new. You think back years ago— software and hardware combined for future growth in both areas. RCA, many years ago, was intent on selling television sets; particularly color TV sets. Well, they owned NBC. They were the first to tell all the producers in Hollywood to

make all the television programs in color. The color
programs worked well and got good ratings and obviously
enhanced and spurred the sale of the color TV sets. RCA
also owned RCA Records. This helped them sell
phonographs, which was the hardware aspect of the
company. So, there's really nothing new under the sun.
That's what I'm saying vis-à-vis the software–hardware
alliances. I think this is just a continuation of what has been
going on for years in the entertainment industry, but on a
much bigger scale, on a global scale. The future looks like it
is going to be one based on international dealings. That goes
on today. I think that we've been vaulted on to center stage
in the international community.

Al Rush
Former Chairman
MCA Television Group

Before the MCA–Matsushita deal, the $5 billion acquisition of
Columbia Pictures Entertainment by Sony Corporation was the
biggest Japanese–American consolidation. Since the Sony–Co-.
lumbia deal took place in 1989, it is now possible to glimpse the
real meaning of words like synergy and vertical-integration. Sony
has financed the construction of the first, state-of-the-art, high-
definition, post-production conversion facility on Columbia's Cul-
ver City studio property. Sony has denied, in testimony before
the U.S. House Telecommunications and Finance Subcommittee,
that it is trying to muscle its HD-TV standard into the Hollywood
production business. Sony, which pioneered digital audio tape
(DAT) technology and created the consumer products which play
DAT cassettes, has started selling DAT versions of its CBS record
library in Japan. Sony also stands to have tremendous leverage
over both the hardware and the software of what is generically
called "the new information age." The lines separating industrial
and consumer electronics are merging as the technology of computers, video, and audio come together to create multimedia machines
that will allow previously undreamed of interaction between the
user and the programming.

Rupert Murdoch's news corporation completed a financial
restructuring in the beginning of 1991 and appears poised to

exploit the synergies of his worldwide media empire. Murdoch's Fox network in the United States is scheduled to launch a television news service; more than 20 movies are scheduled to be produced at the 20th Century Fox studios; and, British Sky Broadcasting (*B-SKY-B*) is now firmly under the control of News Corp. after losing hundreds of millions of dollars in its fight with British Satellite Broadcasting (BSB).

On top of the financial consolidation of the corporate giants, some smaller deals are fueling the consolidation trend in Hollywood. Carolco Pictures, the owner of the *Rambo* movies, sold 10 percent of its company to Japan's Pioneer Electronics, and 5 percent to France's pay-cable, profit-machine, Canal + . Stonebridge Entertainment, the production company owned by movie star Michael Douglas, is making made-for-television movies with financial backing from RAI-2, the Italian network.

Industry analysts universally perceive the Disney Company to be a fiercely independent American company, a non-candidate for Japanese acquisition. But that has not stopped Disney from opening the doors to part of its interests to Japanese investors. In 1990 Disney created the Touchwood Partnership, a consortium of large U.S. and Japanese banks, and Yamaichi Securities, Japan's largest investment firm. Touchwood is raising $600 million to finance the production of more than 30 movies. Much of the funding will come from Japanese investors who will profit from Japan's liberal tax breaks for limited partnerships.

The continued willingness of Japanese and European companies to pay for a piece of the American action in the global programming business will continue throughout the '90s.

To a lesser degree, American companies are also investing in the future of world television. CapCities/ABC, for example, has invested over $100 million in equity positions in non-U.S. companies. Among others, CapCities owns a piece of Screensport in the United Kingdom, and Tele-Munchen in Germany. Other U.S. companies have jumped on the bandwagon. Disney, Fox, Time-Warner, Turner, and NBC all own equity positions in European companies. Group W Productions owns a piece of the French producer/distributor, Tele Images.

A popular answer [to the question of how new independently produced European television product will be financed] is that there will be an increasing number of coproductions among both European and non-European companies. This approach has been quite successful in the recent past, but there are admitted limitations as to both the topics of such programs and the administrative complexities of working with more than one controlling party.

The true future for coproduction, however, seems to be through direct equity investment or joint venturing of accomplished companies of various nationalities. Thus, a number of U.S. production companies have entered into equity investments with noted U.K. and French production houses. Examples of these include Paramount Pictures' investment in Zenith and Group W Production's and NBC's joint ventures with Tele Images. I would look for this trend to continue, as coproduction becomes institutionalized rather than project-based. Subject to local country legislation not imposing undue restrictions on the foreign ownership or involvement in European production companies for purposes of determining the definition of European programming, established American production, distribution, and broadcast companies will most likely play a major role in such investments and joint ventures.

Joseph Calabrese
O'Melveny & Meyers
Los Angeles

Unanswered Questions

The financial consolidation of programming and distribution companies from the major media markets of the world brings up the question of whether there will be enough room for companies, large and small, corporate and independent, to prosper during the next decade.

My view of the world is that there will be large multinational media giants. Time–Warner immediately comes to mind. Burlusconi certainly fits into that category. I think they will continue to exist and some of them will be successful and some of them won't. I think that does not preclude smaller multimedia companies or single-media companies from existing. If the question is: "Will there be a three-network world economy?" My answer is, no. Does that preclude huge media conglomerates? No. Does that preclude the small guys competing at their own levels? No. I think you're going to find a great diversity just as you do now in the United States. There are a number of small media companies that do very nicely as long as they understand what their competitive niche is.

> Herb Granath
> President
> CapCities/ABC Video
> Enterprises

Whether bigger is better and whether the financial consolidation of the programming business will affect the content and style of programs is one of the major unanswered questions. The general consensus thus far is that content and creativity have not been seriously tampered with yet. However, there is great speculation, particularly within the Hollywood creative community, that the financial consolidation will eventually upset the creative process.

A word of warning for you. Europe now thinks it is the center of the universe again and regards America as increasingly marginal to its concerns. To put it at its most basic, Europe is once more fashionable, America is not. This will have programming implications. The best American product will always have a European market. But, increasingly, the second rate, and very American, will not. The explosion of channels will delay this for a while: To begin with they'll need the sheer volume of the American production system to fill airtime. But, there is less interest in things American than I can ever remember in Europe, and that will eventually be reflected in program choices. The purely American will have less of a market in Europe: The challenge for Hollywood is to become more international in outlook, and content. Over 43 percent of Hollywood's motion picture revenues now come from overseas; the same dependency on foreign revenues is about to happen to your television industry. It will not last unless you adapt to international tastes.

> Andrew Neil
> Editor
> *London Sunday Times*

Many television industry executives feel that the financial consolidation sweeping through the business has already changed the landscape forever, and that it is only a matter of time before the studios and the big three American networks join the merger frenzy. Paramount and Disney are frequently identified as candidates, as is Viacom, the New York-based production/distribution company.

With the proliferation of multi-channel television around the world, the control of programming will actually spread to a larger number of entities. As all sports channels, news channels, local children's channels, and shopping channels develop, there will be more programming and distribution agents dispersing product than was true when these territories only had one or two national channels available. The global corporate buyers will, of course, play a significant role. The Rupert Murdochs, Time–Warners, Sony–Columbias will be in evidence in every corner of the television business as the decade rolls on.

> Frank Mancuso
> Former Chairman and CEO
> Paramount Pictures

Whatever changes result from the financial consolidation, there is little doubt that opportunity will abound.

Chapter Fifteen

The New Marketing

The emergence of global television in the '80s has had a profound effect on the advertising and marketing community throughout the world. With the creation of global media companies comes the seductive potential of world-market products. In Europe and Asia, the exponential increase in private television networks has unleashed a flood of new advertising for consumer goods and services. In the United States, continued fractionalization of the mass audience has left advertisers and agencies frantically searching for the most efficient and effective way to motivate consumers to buy their products.

The United States is by far the biggest commercial marketplace in the world. In 1991, experts estimated total advertising in the United States exceeded $135 billion. That represents nearly half of the $290 billion spent on advertising worldwide. Television advertising in the United States, which includes network, cable, syndication, national spot, and local, is projected to be about $35 billion in 1991. To put the television figure in perspective: Western Europe, which has more than 125 million more people than the United States, generates about $16 billion in television advertising revenue—about half the amount generated in the United States. America's robust and mature television market serves as the commercial model for the world.

Advertising in the U.S.

No advertising medium has ever been as successful in selling products and services to consumers as television has. But as domestic television becomes more fractionalized, advertising and marketing experts face the next decade with greater challenges than at any other time in the history of the industry.

> I believe that television will become more personalized either through the dimension of pay-per-view or through something like interactive television; something that will, in effect, segment the medium significantly more than it is targeting now. One of the networks ran a program in which they really attacked the advertising business. One of the boogie-men they put out in this whole area is the fact that advertisers are targeting; as if there is something vicious and subversive about targeting to certain age groups. They held that up as if it was something that was subliminally destructive. I think they ain't seen nothin' yet. Targeting to specific interest areas, like sports, or to specific age categories, or even to specific advertiser interest elements, like automobile advertisers being able to target people who are specifically in the market to buy an automobile, is going to have a major impact on the business. The ability to identify viewers and their interests and to be able to segment more specifically and more accurately will, to a great extent, create the tracks that

programming and that networks will run on. We've already started that in the cable business: the financial network, the black network, the sports network. As the age continuum of the country broadens and you have more and more older people, it's going to be absolutely necessary for advertisers to be able to find ways and means of targeting their messages to people who are interested in their products at a time that they're interested in them. I think there is going to be a significantly increased understanding of the consumer and his and her habits, and opportunities for communicating your sales messages.

> Ike Herbert
> Executive Vice President
> Coca-Cola Company

Domestic advertisers started the '90s with a case of high anxiety. Their clients are cutting marketing budgets in reaction to the general slowdown in consumer spending resulting from the economic recession, and they are questioning the efficiency of television advertising as audiences grow smaller and more fragmented.

What is the logical outgrowth of the fragmented, multi-channel, viewer-is-in-charge-of-what's-going-on, environment? If you know that people are doing a lot of channel switching and flipping and grazing, and you see that ratings are going down, and if you realize that channel switching in cable homes is more than in non-cable homes, you say: Gee, I'm out there in all this stuff but what's the likelihood that anybody is seeing my ads? What's the likelihood that it's doing any good? Then you have all of these other things that are developing, some of which have a high-tech sound to them. Somebody says: I have the ability to target better. Then advertisers say: Gee, this sounds like it might work better. The other reason for the current state of mind of advertisers is that a lot of businesses have become softer. So, in addition to the environment going nuts, I think it's also a matter of people's budgets and salespeople saying: Is this working? They say: My sales are flat. The logical

thing to say is: What am I doing wrong? There is this crazy
television environment now. It's not the way it used to be.
Should I be doing something different? And, how much
should I stay in traditional television? What do I need in
traditional TV versus wherever else I should be in to
augment that? Should I abandon the medium, or should I
find a complement to it?

Jayne Spittler
Vice President & Director of
Media Research
Leo Burnett Advertising

Advertisers cite the increasing cost of advertising on network
television as one of the prominent trends of the '80s.

What is happening in the Super Bowl rates is becoming
unconscionable. There are some very basic concerns about
the cost increases because at a point in time, as media
becomes more and more expensive, you generate a major
barrier to competitive effort. As television becomes more and
more targeted, effective, powerful, and costly, the ability for
new product activity outside of big established firms becomes
more and more difficult. The potential result of that is the
clumping of large companies having more and more impact
on the marketplace, almost a rich get richer kind of thing.
But, clearly it becomes a barrier because it just becomes
unaffordable. If you follow my train of thought and if you'll
grant for the sake of discussion that I'm right, then what
happens is that the networks are now dealing with more and
more powerful advertisers who can begin to dictate to the
television industry what it is they want and on what terms
they want it. You're seeing that to some extent in the retail
grocery trade. The retail grocer is a powerful determinant of
what products are and are not marketed, how they are
marketed, where they are marketed, and under what
circumstances. So, if they end up with fewer and fewer
customers, and those customers begin to generate muscle,
that opens up interesting concerns, it would seem to me. If

these things do, in fact, happen, then they have the potential of being very interesting.

> Ike Herbert
> Executive Vice President
> Coca-Cola Company

Options and Alternatives

From the advertiser's point of view the future of domestic network television is as complicated as it is important.

> One scenario that is out there that nobody talks about much is: does syndication as a delivery form, do the networks as deliverers of programs, eventually go away? If everything can go right into people's homes, do you need the local stations? That's where the FCC comes in. When you look at this future stuff you can't look at it without the regulations that go with it. All these years we've talked about the public interest, convenience, and necessity. And, we have talked about localism. Now that's just going to get swept under the rug by satellite? That's what makes it hard to project where the advertising money will go. If the financial interest and syndication rules were lifted so the networks didn't have to make all of their money off their advertising revenues, maybe they wouldn't have to charge so much money. Maybe network television would become more attractive again. Our experience with syndication and cable is that as the syndication rates go up and cable rates go up we say this isn't as attractive an option to us anymore as network television. Maybe we should just go and buy network television because we're not going to put a premium on any of these other things. Wheel of Fortune is clearing 99 percent of the country and it's producing a wonderful rating. But, if something's clearing 70 percent of the country and is slopped all over the broadcast schedule in terms of its daypart clearance, we're not going to say that that's as imporant to us as something that's on the networks that's clearing 99 percent of the country and is really clearing it when we actually think it is supposed to air. We're not going to take

pains to execute cable with its lower ratings and get it trafficked
and evaluated and everything, if somebody is going to charge
us more money and we don't see any resulting impact for that
money. So, some of this is just efficiency/effectiveness driven.

> Jayne Spittler
> Vice President & Director of
> Media Research
> Leo Burnett Advertising

The programming perspective of the future of domestic mass
market television is driven by many of the same concerns as
those of the advertising community. I asked the former CEO of
one of the major Hollywood studios what forces would impact
his business during the next decade.

The further fractionalizing of viewership with additional
channels provided through cable, DBS, and, potentially,
telephone companies; further pressures on costs as the
competition to attract audiences intensifies; and, significant
regulatory changes that will directly affect the manner in
which production and distribution organizations may merge
or vertically integrate.

> Frank Mancuso
> Former Chairman & CEO
> Paramount Pictures

As mass-market audience shares get smaller, advertisers natu-
rally begin to redefine who the major players are. One of the
biggest industry stories of the late-'80s was the creation and
growth of the Fox television network. Few industry observers
thought Fox had much of a chance of building a national network
of independent affiliates. Probably even fewer thought Fox
would actually evolve into a "fourth" network. I asked Barry
Diller whether he thought the television marketplace at the turn
of the century would be a mass market.

Sure. It'll just not be so obvious. This country has always
been, and will continue to think, more mass than anything

else. It [the mass marketplace] will continue to decline but
not below a certain base level. It's unknown what that might
be. I think it will continue to decline and will, therefore,
allow opportunities for everybody else. There will certainly be
more than three networks. I wouldn't speculate as to how
many. Hopefully, four.

> Barry Diller
> Chairman
> Fox Broadcasting

The Big Three

The big three domestic networks are fighting hard to maintain
their position as television's dominant advertising medium in
the '90s. They are redefining the nature of their relationship
with their advertising clients. Ventures that would never have
been considered seriously in the '80s are now given high priority
as the networks try to increase the value of their commercial
time. In the '90s the networks are doing everything from national mall tours to retail and fast food sweepstakes contests.

- Procter & Gamble, the biggest advertiser on network
  television, has teamed up with CBS to cofinance the production of Northern Exposure. For its help in financing
  production and its commitment to buying half the commercial time in the program, P & G has a minority ownership position in the program.

- ABC runs theme weeks on Good Morning America that
  are designed to attract new advertisers. During these
  weeks, a single-theme series is incorporated into the program and commercial positions are sold to advertisers
  who market products related to the particular theme.

- NBC created a promotion in which viewers were encouraged to play a game that required picking up a game card
  at a Toys 'R Us store and watching an NBC show for
  puzzle clues. In return, Toys 'R Us doubled its expenditures on NBC's Saturday morning schedule.

- AT&T, Visa, Nike, and Sears received special places in a CBS promotional tour which visited malls in 27 different cities. In exchange, CBS received a commitment to purchase a significant amount of commercial time from the group.

- NBC guaranteed General Motors commercial positions in certain shows at more predictable than normal rates for a three-year period in exchange for GM's commercial commitment of more than $500 million.

- CBS and NBC have launched major promotion campaigns for their new fall programming by participating in sweepstakes contests with K mart and McDonald's.

The new commercial openness at the big three networks will likely result in many more historic alliances with advertisers throughout the '90s. As competition whittles down the size of the mass audience, the number of networks that can deliver those new, lower, mass audience figures will increase.

I would venture that five or six years from now you are looking at at least one, probably one other, for a total of about five to six primary suppliers of competitive original programming. I think the market could bear that. Seeing what Fox has done, it's not going to stop here. There will be others entering because the independent stations, more than we, have to compete against Fox on a daily basis. They're not going to sit there with movie reruns as if nothing has changed in the world. They're going to have to get more original and more competitive, and there will be new program supply sources, be it a studio or a consortium of stations pooling their money and going out and buying programming. They're going to have to in order to maintain the kind of footing they had four or five years ago. They're going to have to step up the level of originality in their program bank in prime time.

Brandon Tartikoff
Chairman, Paramount Pictures
Former Chairman, NBC
Entertainment

Barter

During the '80s the syndication, or barter, business experienced phenomenal growth as an advertiser medium. Starting at nearly zero at the beginning of the decade, it became a billion-dollar business by the end of the '80s. Most analysts predict it will continue to grow, at a smaller rate, during the '90s. Ultimately, the health of barter is dependent on the health of network, cable, and other dimensions of the advertising marketplace.

> How much money is going to go into syndication is more difficult to predict. It's been growing by leaps and bounds. The properties that have really been growing are the strong ones. The mid to lower properties are kind of taking it on the chin. Part of the future will depend on how hard-nosed the syndicators are in terms of how they package their programs.
>
> Jayne Spittler
> Vice President & Director of
> Media Research
> Leo Burnett Advertising

Cable

Advertisers are also expected to support continued growth in the cable side of the business during the '90s. Some local market interconnects are becoming aggressive competitors for advertising dollars that, up until recently, have all gone to television. In its December 1990 issue, *Channels* magazine reported a story about a cable interconnect named Bay Cable Advertising (BCA), serving the San Francisco, Oakland, and San Jose marketplace. BCA reportedly racked up $12 million in local ad sales in 1990 by offering advertisers a variety of options. For example, advertisers are able to buy time on certain targeted systems which serve specific neighborhoods. BCA's sales strategy also involves selling the specific niche-appeal of certain cable networks, like ESPN and MTV. Cable will undoubtedly continue to chip away at advertising revenues both nationally and locally.

Advertising on cable is going to go up, and it will have an effect on network revenues. Tarnished though the television environment may be, people are going to say that of all my choices, this still seems to be where some of my money should be going. So much depends on programming and on people's availability. I think we will see more money going into cable. We now have the ability to do some delivery kinds of analysis. We have just done one that looks at how much of your budget you can put into cable in terms of affecting reach, frequency, and delivery. It seems that cable actually can really complement a network. So, I can take 15 percent of my budget and put it in cable. I haven't hurt the network at all and I've actually helped my overall schedule. Because people have the research tools, that's going to happen.

> Jayne Spittler
> Vice President & Director of
> Media Research
> Leo Burnett Advertising

New Opportunities

In the recessionary environment of the early '90s there are some experimental projects that may provide a glimpse into what some advertisers will become involved in during the course of the decade.

There is the one-stop-shopping approach that may be possible for some advertisers working with the new media giants. Chrysler and Time–Warner have announced a marketing arrangement that includes special issues of *Fortune, People,* and *Life* magazines, in which Chrysler will be the exclusive advertiser. Some future Warner Brothers movies will use Chrysler cars in the production. Chrysler will also use Warner Brothers records and Time–Life video for promotions and merchandising. The companies also report that the potential exists for them to use the Warner Brothers and Lorimar Productions units to make special television programs, like the Chrysler showcase series, in which Chrysler sponsors made-for-TV movies.

The *Wall Street Journal* reports that giant multimedia marketing packages are also being prepared for potential clients by the Turner Broadcasting System and the Gannett Company.

A number of coventures between television production companies and magazines have been announced. For the magazines the goal is to increase circulation and to attract major advertisers who normally would not place advertisements in highly specialized publications. For the networks and cable networks, the specials offer an opportunity to target very specific audiences with attractive reality-based programming.

- *Premier*, the monthly movie magazine, produces behind-the-scene specials for Fox Broadcasting.

- *People* magazine, with Bristol-Myers as the sponsor, produces People on TV specials for CBS.

- *Outside* magazine has produced two adventure specials for ABC Sports.

- *Esquire* is teamed up with the Lifetime cable network for a weekly series called: Esquire: About Men and Women.

Advertisers are going to be ever more concerned with the question of where is the right place for them to spend their money. What blend of highly targeted media and mass media do I have to put together for me to be the most effective? How much of a direct marketing effort do I use? Right now, everybody is kind of off on a let's-get-more-targeted approach. If they can reach women in doctors' offices that sounds more targeted than what they do in conventional TV. So, they say, let's go do that. Now we're really into apples and oranges. We're calling it "placed TV," the Whittle and CNN stuff in schools. The Whittle stuff in doctors' offices. The check-out channel stuff in supermarkets. How do you evaluate that stuff? Since there isn't much money going into placed TV now, there will be a substantial increase in the future. There is an early novelty to it. Because, there's a growing concern about whether TV is really doing it for me anymore. This sounds good. So, I'll go do it. Depending on what kind of numbers come back or on what kinds of results happen, people will reevaluate that.

Jayne Spittler
Vice President & Director of
Media Research
Leo Burnett Advertising

In the '90s advertisers will continue to experiment with new media vehicles that are trying to create markets that did not even exist ten years ago.

CHAPTER SIXTEEN

Television Marketing: Europe

The deregulation of broadcasting in Europe, and the subsequent increase in the number of European television stations, created not only a tremendous market demand for programming. It was also the catalyst for geometric growth in the television advertising business. By the early '90s most of the new stations in Europe had made their huge bulk purchases of start-up programming. The so-called boom in program purchasing was over and distributors began to face a much more competitive marketplace where decisions to purchase programs were being made much like they are in the United States.

Advertising in Europe

In the advertising dimension of Europe's new television industry, most experts project that the boom times may have just begun. At the 1990 media summit in Luxembourg, John Perriss, the worldwide media director for Saatchi and Saatchi Communications, presented his company's forecasts for advertising growth in Europe. First, he compared the real growth rate, after inflation, in various regions of the world. The U.S. market was projected to grow about 5 percent by 1992. In the same period, Europe was projected to grow by 20 percent. The projected growth rates of certain individual markets were even more stunning. France was projected to grow by 20 percent, Germany by 46 percent, and Spain by 90 percent! Following John Perriss, a second distinguished speaker addressed the crowd and left no doubt about where he felt the European advertising market was headed.

> In 1980, the United States spent almost four times as much as all of Europe on television advertising. By 1990, the United States spent only twice as much. Where will it go in the '90s? I think that the growth in Europe will continue at double the United States rate. By the end of the century, Europe and the United States will be close to parity in total television ad spending. In France in 1980 there were only three channels. This grew to 22 channels by 1990. Television advertising growth was even more impressive. It rose from only $360 million in 1980 to an estimated $2.1 billion in 1990. Why this explosion in Europe? Because the deregulation of ownership has been implemented, and because countries have loosened restrictions on the amount of advertising. The liberalizing of ownership, programming rules, and advertising time now allows for successful commercial ventures in television. The growth in channels stimulates ad spending.
>
> Thomas Reifenheiser
> Senior Vice President
> Chase Manhattan Bank

In 1990, the *New York Times* wrote a trend piece that quoted several top executives at major advertising agencies speculating that Europe would become such a hot growth market that eventually a number of U.S. agencies would move their headquarters to London or the continent. The piece went on to report on the chairman and CEO of D'Arcy, Masius, Benton & Bowles who was temporarily moving his office to London so that he could be closer to the action.

> If you take advertising pounds per head, we're a long way behind the United States in Europe. I think there is a major opportunity because a lot of the markets in Europe are pretty underdeveloped in terms of television advertising. In Holland, for example, not so long ago you were only allowed to buy two spots a week. That was it. And, you couldn't say where the spot went. That doesn't exactly encourage advertisers to use the medium. As you get private channels and opportunities arising for advertising, you will, of course, get more money being spent on television advertising. There's a lot spent in the press, for example. And, there's a lot spent on other areas of marketing which may lead to more money going above the line and more money going into TV. There is a great opportunity to at least come up with a per capita figure which is more close to the U.S. figure than we are now.
>
> Brian Jacobs
> Vice-Chairman & Executive
> Media Director
> Leo Burnett Limited, London

Advertising revenues from Europe already exceed those from the United States at many international ad agencies. With inter-country trade barriers coming down in 1992, the big agencies are reorganizing their corporate structures so they can better serve their clients. Grey Advertising, for example, has reportedly created a new European board of executives to service their clients' European campaigns. J. Walter Thompson has also reportedly set up a London-based management unit to handle pan-European advertising strategies. This unit manages marketing, media, and research projects for its clients who are doing business throughout Europe. There is even a version of agency

coproduction which has been announced. BBDO Worldwide
and DDB Needham Worldwide have reportedly joined up with
Ogilvy & Mather Worldwide to form a European media buying
entity called The Media Partnership. This unit will service the
European media requirements for the clients of all three companies.

During the 1990 media summit, one of Europe's most influential advertising executives spent some time giving insight into
the new European advertising market and finished his remarks
with a sobering warning.

> We can't talk anymore about a mass consumer. We are now
> talking about the "I am me" consumer. As he has the
> choice, is better educated and better informed, he insists on
> his personal decisions. He chooses as an individual and not
> as part of the masses. Because of this consumer
> demassification, or individualization, the role of advertising
> has changed. Up to the '70s the role of advertising was to
> inform and convince the consumer to buy our products. The
> consumer has rejected this role of advertising. He doesn't
> want a hard sell. The new role of advertising has become:
> "To seduce and understand me as a consumer. And, maybe
> I will like you then." This has forced manufacturers into a
> much more indirect advertising approach. Advertising
> without entertainment values and emotions are simply
> rejected by consumers. This also means that advertising is
> focusing more on creating a relationship between the brand
> and the consumer. The product really becomes the tangible
> proof of the brand positioning and image. The brand has
> become the link between the product and the consumer.
> That's why brands are so valuable today. The brand helps
> the consumer make the right choice. The brand helps the
> consumer to diminish risk. The brand is not a rational entity
> but an emotional one. What does all this lead to? It just
> points out that advertising as part of total marketing
> spending has lost its dominance as the only selling tool to the
> consumer and its costs are growing out of proportion. But,
> let me be clear. I'm not saying that advertising is not
> important. To the contrary. It is our strongest brand
> positioning tool. But, all the other elements in the marketing

mix have gained importance, like trade marketing, promotions, sponsorship, packaging, direct marketing, licensing, programming, etc. In the '60s, an average of 64 percent of marketing budgets were spent in media advertising. Today, this has fallen to an average of about 35 percent. As an example, in Japan, Nescafé ran a major campaign to 15–20 year olds for three years. Not one traditional media vehicle was used. We could not afford to use television. This leads to my first caution: Those who are making forecasts that media advertising spending will triple over the next ten to twenty years might be sadly mistaken, and those who are building big projects based on those projected revenues might be in for nasty surprises.

> Michel Reinarz
> Director of Visual
>   Communications
> Nestlé

Barter

The barter business, which grew from practically nothing into a billion-dollar-a-year business in the United States during the '80s, is in its infancy in Europe. Experts are hesitant to speculate about its long-term prospects. One trend that favors the growth of barter is the increase in the number of European television stations. Some of these stations may be receptive to trading inventory in return for programming. Another encouraging trend is the overall growth of television advertising throughout Europe. But most experts, when asked to speculate about barter in Europe, focus on the things that make it difficult. Larry Lammatina, of EC TV, is one American-based executive who is having success with barter in France.

It depends on the programs. I don't think there is a big future for marginal programming on marginal stations in marginal time periods. I don't think barter is going to be very successful in that area for the simple reason that European stations can buy all the marginal programming

they want from American producers at very attractive prices.
Where the marketplace really heats up and is active is on
hits. Television has been and will always be a hit business. If
you have what is perceived to be a hit then you are in a
better position to negotiate a higher price and you're in a
better position to influence the terms of business. After
Wheel of Fortune was established here in the States with the
stations, our friends King World said your cash price is going
up a little but, more importantly, we're putting a minute of
our own commercials in there. Some stations liked it. Some
didn't. But, they wanted a show that did a 15 or 20 rating
and they basically said OK. And, King World said we want
you to sign up for two years. And, they said OK. But if it
was doing a three rating, I think the stations might have
said: we don't want to do that. So, everything starts with the
program. Whereas in the past, in the United States, there
was a lot of barter for marginal programs, for marginal time
periods, I don't think we're going to see a lot of that over the
long term in Europe. New stations, just starting out, trying
to keep their cash, wanting to broadcast for a full broadcast
day, are seeing virtually no advertising revenue in the early
morning or late at night. They might do barter deals just to
fill up their airwaves at the lowest possible price. Beyond
that, I don't think you'll see it happen.

Larry Lammatina
President
EC TV

There is a general agreement that barter, as it is known in the
United States, is, at best, a long way off. However, since there
is so little of it in Europe today, it is bound to increase significantly on a percentage basis throughout the next decade. Most
barter deals will likely be highly customized to benefit the advertiser and the station.

You have a lot of laws in certain countries. You may sell an
event to Coke, for example, who would then take that and
trade it for time on a network where the time might not run
in the show. We think of barter, usually, in the States, as

being client-furnished programming with their commercials running in the show. But, you can also barter shows for time and the time can appear elsewhere on the network. I would say it'll be a hybrid because it very much varies with the countries and their rules and how commercialized they are. You have to realize that the barter business didn't exist ten years ago. So, you have a completely different group of people who have seen a billion-dollar-a-year business rise in the last decade, who are still the ones who created it. And, so, it's an industry that's still staffed by pioneers who are looking for new territories to conquer. It's a slightly different mindset. Also, you've got Europeans who have watched the rise of this and understand that they are making major transitions in their own broadcasting structure, and they are looking to America to learn both what to do and what not do do. They see barter as a way to reduce their cash outlay for programming. And, you see advertisers. Basically, anything that allows them to get advertising on for less money is very important to them because it goes straight to the bottom line. So, you have a couple of forces that are very eager to see barter grow and develop.

> Michael Garin
> Senior Managing Director
> Furman, Selz

Sponsorship

Although the barter business is generally perceived as being very difficult in Europe, many experts feel comfortable predicting a rosy future for program sponsorship. As is the case with barter, there is very little sponsorship done in Europe now, but there are market forces that seem to be encouraging for its development.

Although sponsorship is a concept widely used in the United States to produce and distribute television programming, its use in Europe is relatively new. Despite current prohibition in some countries and some initial problems, sponsorship will undoubtedly play a larger role in European television production in the future. Although the EC television directive and local country legislation provide often strict guidelines for sponsorship, its increasing popularity with broadcasters and producers has already led to more innovative approaches, and, in some countries, to the relaxation of certain restrictions. France and Italy are two countries that have liberalized sponsorship rules and that are experiencing a rapid increase in sponsorship revenues. The future of sponsorship in Europe, therefore, seems clear.

Joseph Calabrese, Esq.
O'Melveny & Meyers

What I think you're going to see more of than anything else is sponsorship. You're going to see advertising agencies buying the rights to something like Wheel of Fortune, which they have already done, and producing it and clearing time on stations throughout Europe and putting their own clients in. You're going to see some of that. Or, they would give the program for nothing in exchange for time. And they'll take 2½ minutes and they'll leave the station 2½ minutes. So, the station doesn't pay anything for the program and they have the rights to sell 2½ minutes themselves. But, I definitely think it will be on a country-by-country basis because there is enormous nationalism in each country. There are different time periods, different structures, etc., etc. It's much easier to do it in the United States because you're dealing with one country.

Michael Solomon
President
Warner Bros. International

Research Techniques

As television advertising expands geometrically throughout the decade in Europe, more and more attention will be devoted to research techniques. Although there are various approaches to measuring and analyzing audiences throughout Europe, there is no standardized approach for the European Community at large.

> Another major issue will be research, and particularly media research. It is inconceivable that we are pushing for the United States of Europe and blaming the politicians for pussy-footing around with solving the technical and financial barriers while the industry has not been able to harmonize media research techniques, data, and definitions. It is even more appalling to know that no united Europe is necessary to set common standards for research. There is no legal justification, only the ''not-invented-here'' syndrome. It wouldn't be a bad idea to challenge ourselves through professional associations to have full harmonization in media research before January 1, 1993. Then we can stop blaming politicians, until we have proven that we can achieve this goal outside legislation. I might even go a step further. There is today not one single research technique which tells me how many and which people actually see my TV or radio spot or my print ad. And I thought that was what media research was about. We are still only guessing today. We are still using techniques based on assumptions of thirty years ago. It might have been enough to measure the audience at the end of a program and at the beginning of the next to have a reasonable idea of the ratings of your spot. Today, the advertising clutter, long blocks, remote control, and program choice make this measurement irrelevant. Some exploratory, but contentious, research has indicated loss of audiences by more than 50 percent during advertising breaks. Therefore, I believe we need to set top priority on obtaining new audience research which gives us more accurate information.
>
> Michel Reinarz
> Director of Visual
> Communication
> Nestlé

The new, sophisticated realities of international marketing require that programmers, as well as advertisers, need contemporary, state-of-the-art research tools. A new American company, International Ratings Services (IRS), is the first company to provide U.S. programming clients periodic ratings performance reports from the major European countries. With a variety of distribution clients including CBS Broadcast International, Warner Brothers, and Columbia, IRS serves as a middleman, working with the local audience measurement companies in each of the European markets. It collects and processes the data for distribution to its American programming clients. European research companies working with IRS include AGB in the United Kingdom and Italy, GfK in Germany, Mediametre in France, and Ecotel in Spain. International programming executives unanimously predict that, in the '90s, effective marketing of American programs in Europe will rely just as heavily on quality local research data as it does in the mature and competitive U.S. market.

Global Advertising

The longer you gaze into the marketing crystal ball, the more likely you are to focus in on global advertising. The concept has tantalized marketing and advertising people for many years. Will it be possible, in an electronically connected world, to use satellites in such a way that the same commercial message is beamed around the globe? With a few notable exceptions, the promise of global advertising has eluded marketers thus far. But now a number of media professionals from throughout the world think that we just might be on the verge of a dramatic explosion of global advertising. They see signs pointing to the eventual emergence of global advertising in all four corners of the earth. Saatchi and Saatchi, the British-based agency which is one of the largest in the world, has been hired by Gosteleradio to plan and strategize the commercial future of television in Russia. Even with a very underdeveloped consumer economy the U.S.S.R. has nearly 200 million television viewers.

Imagine the commercial opportunities ten, or fifteen, or twenty years down the road, in an emerging market of 200 million. Warner Brothers International has what may be the most unusual barter deal in the world in China. Programs like Hunter and Falcon Crest are supplied to the Chinese television system in return for commercial time in the programs. Warner Brothers then sells that advertising inventory to Western companies who want to begin building brand awareness for their products in China. They are betting that some day China will begin to develop a consumer economy. When those Warner Brothers programs air in China they are seen by a mere 450 million people! Some marketing experts whose products are universal have detected a worldwide convergence of consumer psychographics that is happening in tandem with the building of the infrastructure of the global electronic village.

> As far as global marketing for a vast number of products is concerned, I think that it is inescapable. It is already beginning to happen. What research is turning up more and more in more and more product categories in the developed world is that the similarities of consumers are so much more of a fact than their dissimilarities were five or ten years ago. The homogenization of consumer attitudes, primarily through exposure to mass media, will continue and will evolve and it will not be very long before, in a large number of categories, you're going to have common consumers throughout the world. If you zero in on Europe, for example; distribution is not our problem. The problem up until now has been the fragmentation of the media.
>
> If we get to the point where we can cover the EC with two or three television networks, like we do here in the United States, where you have common currency, where you generate common package labeling requirements, what you really begin to do is you homogenize that marketplace and you begin to reach the market even more effectively than we are doing now.
>
> Ike Herbert
> Executive Vice President
> Coca-Cola Company

Some executives predict that global advertising, by its very nature, will be a very small part of the overall advertising pie. They point out that the style of such ads would have to be almost entirely visual, perhaps with music, because of the obvious language barriers. Others point out that values and lifestyles in different parts of the world will render global advertising useless for many products. But the prospect of a giant, world advertising market is irresistible for many.

> Global advertising is certainly going to increase. How much is hard to tell. It's going to increase because cable formats that are going to be exported around the world are going to have to be supported in some way. They'll either have to be supported through user fees or through advertising, or a combination of the two the way cable networks work here in the United States. Unquestionably there will be an increase in global advertising. Now, whether it will be truly global or more regional; it will probably be more regional. There's not a whole lot of business right now in South America or Africa or, say, the Indian subcontinent. But Europe is another story. But, there you have the language problem. There will definitely be more of it. How much more is anybody's guess. We'll just have to wait and see.
>
> Ted Turner
> Chairman
> Turner Broadcasting System

The degree to which global advertising prospers during the '90s will depend, to some extent, on the types of programs created for the world market. In July of 1990 an Italian company named Sacis handled the worldwide satellite distribution of a concert which originated in Rome. Three of the world's greatest opera singers, Luciano Pavarotti, Placido Domingo, and José Carreras, were featured. Forty-six percent of the people watching television in Italy were watching. Audiences in the United States, Hungary, Poland, Czechoslovakia, Europe, and most of Latin America also watched the program. For the U.S.S.R. distribution of the concert, Sacis put together a barter deal whereby an Italian company named Ferruzzi, which is in the agriculture business, paid for the satellite costs and the Russian market rights in return for advertising in the program. It was, reportedly, the first time that a Western company paid for the Soviet TV rights in return for advertising on Soviet television.

Global advertising is an old issue that's been kicking around
for a long time. It really depends on what the advertiser is
trying to do. What kind of products does the advertiser have?
What kind of organization does the advertiser want to
maintain? There are examples of people moving in that
direction and there are examples of people moving away from
it. Colgate just fired its international advertising group whose
job was to make commercials that would work across the
world. They have now disavowed that. They've said: we
ain't doing that anymore. It's a local issue. The local people
will have autonomy. They will make the advertisements.
We'll no longer attempt to do global advertising. On the
other hand, there are other advertisers of certain products
that do have a global positioning and global market who are
going in that direction. It really depends on the situation and
the advertiser of the product. Language is very important.
When you see a company like Coke, you could say that they
are global advertisers. They have a fairly simple message.
Their advertising tends to be very visual. They are a global
advertiser. Johnny Walker is trying to do that. Marlboro was
certainly the cowboy all over the world. Wherever you go,
you see the same basic approach. I think that when you look
at certain luxury goods, the positioning is pretty much the
same and the advertising is pretty much the same across the
world. It's targeted against a certain segment of the market,
the top five or ten percent, and those people tend to be more
similar around the world than, say, the lower 25 percent. If
you are a certain kind of advertiser with a certain kind of
product, global advertising may be the entire pie. If you're a
different kind of advertiser with a different kind of product, it
may be zero percent of the pie. It sounds like a dodge. But,
as in most things in advertising and marketing, it depends.

> Larry Lammatina
> President
> EC TV

A number of major agency executives agree that the big international shops will operate simultaneously on both a global/
regional, and a national basis by the turn of the century. They

describe the global television marketplace as one where advertisers do not buy programs, they rent audiences.

> I think that what it means is basically a uniformity of opportunity and greater opportunity for advertisers everywhere to use TV as a medium for their purposes rather than simply as a way of giving money to broadcasters. As the opportunities proliferate and the new TV stations grow and are hopefully successful, advertisers will be able to advertise more efficiently, and as a result their business will grow and the world will happily continue to spin. What has traditionally happened is that you haven't had that uniformity of opportunity. Because, for example, you've had markets where you could only buy two spots a week. And, there's not a whole lot you're going to be able to do with that. So, as the private TV stations grow and as the U.S. companies and other companies are successfully providing them with programs, and as they continue to deliver big audiences, mixed audiences with different ages and so on, advertisers will be able to benefit because they will be able to reach the people they want to reach much more effectively and efficiently. I think that's what the global marketplace means from our perspective and that's why for us over here we certainly very much welcome it. It will mean that we have greater opportunities to sell our wares and practice our skills.

Brian Jacobs
Vice Chairman & Executive
Media Director
Leo Burnett Limited, London

Global selling requires the packaging of audiences, not shows. Even though there is considerable debate about how important it will be in the future, most advertising executives are comfortable with the concept of the global marketplace.

CHAPTER SEVENTEEN

U.S. Public Policy

At the beginning of the 21st century, the nature of the television business, both domestically and internationally, will partially be the result of public policy decisions made in Washington, D.C., during the '90s. Public policy can either stimulate or retard new, market-driven developments. In retrospect, for example, it is clear that the deregulating of the domestic cable industry in the '80s was the catalyst for tremendous growth in the cable sector. The implementing of the prime-time access rule can be credited with stimulating exponential growth in the program production business during the '80s.

The FCC

The Federal Communications Commission faces a number of critical policy challenges at the start of the '90s. Should the networks now be allowed to own and/or distribute their programs? Should the cable industry now be reregulated? How can high-definition television best be introduced as the new technical standard for television pictures?

The answers to these and other questions will require the support and the blessing of Al Sikes, who was sworn in as chairman of the FCC in August of 1989.

In short order, Chairman Sikes demonstrated that during his tenure at the helm of the nation's communications regulatory agency he would aggressively orchestrate the evolution of America's public policy.

Actually, Sikes began working on the future of television during the mid-'80s when he was an assistant secretary in the U.S. Department of Commerce and the administrator of the National Telecommunications and Information Administration, known as the N.T.I.A. In that job, he supervised a major government project called "Telecom 2000: Charting the Course for a New Century." The Telecom 2000 project involved dozens of government staff experts and more than 70 professional representatives from the communications industries. It was the first comprehensive review of the U.S. communications and information businesses since President Johnson ordered what became known as the Rostow Task Force back in 1968. The recommendations made by the Rostow Task Force became the foundation of the country's Open Sky policy which, among many other advances, supported the development and growth of our contemporary satellite communications system.

The conclusions and recommendations of the Telecom 2000 project are the foundation and the framework of government communications policy in the '90s. This is how the report begins:

As America progresses toward the 21st century, the horizon offers vistas of matchless promise, potential, and opportunities. New technologies, embodied in commercial innovation and driven by the economic engine of competitive enterprise, can help satisfy our nation's critical needs in new ways. The resulting services can contribute to building a more creative, productive, and humane American society. Today *is* the information age, and telecommunications comprises its chief transportation system. Invisible high-

ways of fiber-optic cable and radio waves each second carry
trillions of bits of information vital to the smooth function-
ing of our economy and society. Telecommunications is the
electronic tie which can more closely bind our nation of communities together into an electronic national neighborhood. Telecommunications affords individuals expanded
access to information. In fundamental ways, it thus offers
the individual greater freedom, and more social and economic power. By capitalizing on these electronic resources
more effectively, America has an opportunity to become
more competitive while enriching the overall quality of our
national life. The electronic tools of the information age—
personal computers and videocassette recorders, for example—already have transformed most of our lives. They offer
yet untapped potential to expand personal opportunities, to
foster creativity, and, hence, contribute to individual freedom, more perhaps, than followed the advent of the auto-
mobile less than a century ago. Appreciating these opportunities, and capitalizing upon them, however, will require
greater understanding and a stronger national communications policy consensus.

What is the proper role of government in shaping the future of
television? Here is what the Telecom 2000 report said:

Yesterday's institutional arrangements have lost and will
continue to lose relevance in the face of technical and commercial developments. Domestically, arrangements dating
from 1934 and passage of the Communications Act may
handicap the introduction of technology, as occurred with
cellular mobile telephone and cable television service. Today, a judicial regulatory bottleneck is affecting the wider
and more effective distribution of information age benefits.
Yet, internationally, government has inescapable responsibilities and must be better organized to fulfill them. We face
a promising future filled with dazzling new technologies and
applications, but our achievement of maximum benefit
from this electronic cornucopia may be compromised by
unnecessary or ineffective government actions. Domestic
regulatory costs, which were bad enough when America en-
joyed unchallenged economic leadership, have clear poten-

tial to impose unacceptable burdens as we strive to maintain
our national competitiveness. Internationally, the time
when we could afford the current dispersion of government
responsibilities is gone. How we tackle such difficulties will
be a major challenge as we progress toward the 21st century.

Chairman Sikes' response to the question of the role of government in the emerging global communications industry is a
little more specific.

> Government, in brief, should first seek to encourage
> competition and individual opportunity, to rely to the
> maximum extent possible to ensure competitive
> free-enterprise communications markets provide customers
> the options and choices they want and are willing to pay for.
> Second, where important public policy goals are identified,
> which markets will not adequately further, government
> should be prepared to advance those goals in the least
> intrusive, most target-efficient manner.

> Al Sikes
> Chairman
> Federal Communications
> Commission

Clearly, the regulatory climate in the early '90s supports the
concept of open, market-driven competition. There is the veiled
threat that if the government concludes that the development
of a particular dimension of the business is not occurring fast
enough, it will use its regulatory muscle to stimulate growth.
These are the principles that have led many industry experts
to conclude that the regional telephone companies will eventually be in the television program delivery business.

Program Delivery

In March of 1991, members of the U.S. Telephone Association
and National Association of Broadcasters began what is expected
to be an on-going series of meetings in Washington. The televi-

sion representatives want to ensure that local TV stations are favorably treated if, and when, the phone companies begin delivering programming via high-tech, fiber-optic lines. The phone companies reportedly feel that their case for entry into the program delivery business will be strengthened if they reach an operational agreement that is acceptable to the TV stations. Undoubtedly, many cable companies will oppose the entry of the phone companies. Insight into the resolution of the issue can be found in the Telecom 2000 document.

> Just as the Open Sky policy of the 1970s increased satellite telecommunications competition, improving quality and reducing costs, and thereby enhancing the electronic fabric of our economic and social life, similar open entry for local alternative network providers, cable television service, direct broadcast satellite, teleports, multichannel multipoint distribution systems, and technologies not yet known, will enhance the development of a vastly improved infrastructure. The role of regulation should be deemphasized and instead the focus should be on the critical need for enhancement of the telecommunications and information infrastructure.

As if to demonstrate the role cable television plays in their future business strategy, five of the seven Baby Bell companies are currently spending billions of dollars building cable systems in the United Kingdom, Israel, and France. In many of those European projects the Bell companies are partnered with U.S. cable companies.

Observers speculate that the Bell companies are working with the cable operators in Europe to show Washington regulators and U.S. industry leaders that they can be supportive, rather than threatening, players in cable television. The phone companies have focused their challenge to be allowed into the domestic cable business on the issue of other high-tech services which they say will be available if they are allowed to participate. This is the so-called "one-wire, super-system" that offers consumers voice, data, facsimile, video-on-demand, and video-conferencing.

It is the transportation system which the technology futurists say is necessary for the ultimate merger of video, audio, and computers into the multimedia communications world of to-morrow.

> Fiber-optic delivery systems radically alter the traditional cost equation associated with the provision of both familiar and new "broadband" communications services. By sharply reducing the cost of communications, such systems also affect the demand for, and price of, associated equipment. Much of the U.S. intercity communications network already has been largely converted to fiber-optics; the technology is increasingly used in intracity trunk lines; the economics of deploying fiber to the curb, and potentially, to the home, should change quickly this decade.

> Al Sikes
> Chairman
> Federal Communications
> Commission

The Telecom 2000 report makes clear its position on traditional television broadcasting.

> Over-the-air broadcasting should remain a vital element of the national media mix, as few industries have demonstrated so consistent a talent and ability to deliver what the public and advertisers want. Broadcast television may experience further structural changes. Communications history, however, provides almost no instances in which an established business well-serving the public was actually eclipsed. It is conceivable that television may prove less profitable, but there is no good reason to assume that in coming years we will experience a market-driven demise of over-the-air video service.

Regulation or Deregulation?

As competition eroded the audience share of traditional broadcasters throughout the '80s, many of the government regulations affecting television stations have been altered or have disappeared. The world does not seem unduly affected by the absence of the fairness doctrine, for example, and government regulators are not finished deregulating television stations. The Telecom 2000 report clearly defines the challenge to develop government policies that better conform to the new reality of a vastly more competitive television environment:

> Television remains the most regulated of electronic mass media. Policymakers must develop a regulatory framework which both recognizes new and evolving marketplace realities and affords broadcasters a full and fair opportunity to compete effectively in an increasingly competitive and dynamic media environment. Where competition can be reasonably expected to function as an effective surrogate for what regulation ideally might accomplish, government should not regulate and reliance should be placed on the marketplace. Additionally, imposing regulatory obligations on one set of players in a competitive marketplace, but not on others, has clear potential to distort the future development of the overall electronic media market. Advertising, for example, constitutes one of the fastest growing sources of cable television system revenue today. Local television and radio stations, as well as national broadcast networks, thus compete increasingly with cable for audiences and advertising dollars. While cable and broadcasters are increasingly competitors in the same market, broadcasters remain subject to federal licensing and other regulations which oblige them to air programming independent of marketplace demand. Reporting and other requirements are also imposed. Consistent with good public policy, government should foster an environment conducive to maximum competition among firms which are similarly situated. Such a competitive market is more likely to ensure that the public has the options it wants and needs than even the most dedicated, well-meaning, conscientious government regulators can reliably accomplish. The predominant focus should be on fostering competition,

however, not tacitly allocating markets or handicapping one or more groups of particular competitors.

In addition to the on-going deregulation of television broadcasting, the industry can expect growth in the direct broadcast satellite business throughout the decade. Chairman Sikes predicts that once high-definition television is introduced in the mid–1990s, it will rapidly become the predominant transmission technique by the turn of the century.

Perhaps the clearest insight into the future of public policy in the United States during the '90s is gleaned from Chairman Sikes' answer to the question of how he would like to see the FCC evaluated in the year 2000.

> The FCC, hopefully, will have made the regulatory adaptations necessary to enable existing communications industry participants to compete, and to permit new goods and service providers to enter the market. Particularly important will be actions which enable customers, including ordinary residential users, expanded access to new service options; and actions which permit the broader and more effective use of telecommunications assets to deliver educational, health care, governmental, and other social services, in addition to those actions which facilitate more effective and efficient use of these "electronic-tools" by business and commerce.

> Al Sikes
> Chairman
> Federal Communications
> Commission

The chairman's answer stresses a bias favoring open-market competition, not protection, and nurturing the development of new emerging technologies.

CHAPTER EIGHTEEN

The New Technologies

Demo. Die. Crash. Burn. These words, printed boldly in black on the white face of a wall-clock have been substituted for the numbers 12, 3, 6, and 9. Whenever a researcher or faculty person at the world famous MIT Media Lab checks the time, he or she is reminded of the rules of the game. In the other halls of academia throughout the country, publication of research work is the most valued accomplishment—publish or perish. At the MIT Media Lab, where the future of television is being created, the rule is: demo or die. The slogan reflects the media lab's uncompromising and absolute commitment to demonstrable results. No speculation allowed here. As the lab's director, Nicholas Negroponte, says: "No voyeurism permitted."

Computers and TV

The media lab is in Cambridge, on the campus of the Massachusetts Institute of Technology, on the north bank of the Charles River. It is housed in a spectacular building that was designed by architect I. M. Pei. When a visitor approaches the media lab building, it is obviously an unusual and special place. This is where the future of television is being invented.

The media lab's broad mission is to explore what computers could be doing ten or twenty years from now. It has become a mecca for people who are interested in the future of computer technology. In the last five years more than 20,000 scientists and business executives have made the pilgrimage to the MIT campus to get a glimpse of the future. Nobody wants to be left out of the loop. Funding to run the lab's multimillion-dollar operation comes from some of the world's most successful communications companies: CapCities/ABC, Apple Computer, CBS, Digital Equipment Corp., IBM, MCA, Mitsubishi, RCA, Sony, Toshiba, Warner Communications, and many other corporate giants.

The roots of the MIT Media Lab go back ten years and are grounded in an idea which, at the time, was considered to be out-of-this-world—the worlds of video and broadcasting, print and publishing, and computers are destined to merge into one technology. Today, the idea is universally accepted.

The media lab was conceived at a time when personal computers did not even exist. Computers were thought of as esoteric and intimidating tools used by scientists. Today, the lab's original vision of the future has become a reality. Computers have integrated many dimensions of our daily lives, and the computer industry is clearly focused on making computers user-friendly for everyone from the expert to the novice. Personal computers have more power today than a room full of mainframes had 15 years ago. Power is growing exponentially while the size of computing devices shrinks. As all this happens, more and more people are using computers. That's really why the media lab exists. It's all about what happens between people and computers and how the process can be simplified and made more relevant.

A *Time* magazine article described the mission of the media lab this way: "To transfer today's passive mass media, particularly TV, into flexible technologies that can respond to individual taste." In the booklet written to celebrate the lab's fifth anniversary, there is more information on what the lab is trying to accomplish:

> By media we mean highly personal and interactive information systems that seek to accommodate the user's interest-level, ability, and current mindset. The computers we are thinking about are more like people. They will not just be passive vessels for the display of whatever materials the mass media feel you might want to see. They will understand context, abstract contents, and use common sense to filter and present for you information in accordance with their understanding of you, your schedule, your mood. The next millennium will be one of personalized media, a concept which has been, to date, an oxymoron.

The work of the media lab is divided into twelve cutting-edge groups. They include: vision and modeling, spatial imaging, interactive cinema, movies of the future, electronic publishing, and television of tomorrow.

At a symposium in October 1990, the lab demonstrated some of the work being done in the department of music and cognition. There was a public performance of a musical piece called *Etudes*. This is how it was described in the conference agenda: "*Etudes* is probably the first piano duet for a single pianist. In addition to the pianist's part, a second part is played on the same piano by a computer which follows the pianist's performance. Bisset [a computer scientist] is playing on an acoustic piano, which has been equipped with a midi input and output. On the Yamaha disklavier piano, each key can be played from the keyboard, but it can also be activated by an electric solenoid within the piano. A Macintosh computer 'listens' to the human performer and controls the piano's response."

If the media lab is right, television in the 21st century will be a very different business. The Television of Tomorrow group describes its vision of the future as open architecture TV.

> Our open architecture television research is exploring the absolute and uncompromising union of computers and

television. We disagree with current conventional thinking about high-definition television, HD-TV, being the next evolutionary step in television, if only because it is not good enough, and today's embodiments are too rooted in analog strategies of the past. Television will be digital, from end to end, before the close of the century.

Digital TV will transmit the audio and video coming into your house in computer language—zeros and ones—instead of the current analog information that is transmitted over the airways. Most experts predict that the way this digital information will get into your house will be over fiber-optic cable installed by the phone company. Digital fiber-optic cable is capable of handling one hundred times the information carried on today's coaxial cable. It will allow consumers to dial-up a virtually unlimited number of TV programs, to transmit live and taped video pictures from their personal TV to other TVs anywhere in the world, and to access enormous libraries of data and information. The living room TV becomes an interactive home computer, but that's just the beginning of the revolution.

In the future, most information will not be sent to people. It will be sent to machines. That is really the fundamental difference. The consequences of that are really quite enormous. Broadcasting is really very interesting. I'm picking broadcasting and computers as my two examples. I'm doing that because, of all the media, the first that will really suffer very seriously is network television. I really believe that it's going to have extraordinary trouble over the next three or four years. One of the reasons is that when television was invented the assumption was, a perfectly good assumption at the time, that you put all the intelligence in the transmitter and fundamentally nothing in the receiver.

By comparison with some of the more modern appliances in your home I bet that most of us have televisions that, on a per-cubic-foot basis, are the dumbest appliances in our homes. We really don't yet put very much computing in the receiver. That is going to change dramatically. The other change is that basically that which we get through the air today we will get through the ground, and that which we get

through the ground we will get through the air. You already
get cable television through the ground and you already have
cellular telephones. That's just the beginning of the trend.
Think about the computer intelligence you can put in a
television receiver. You get at home at night and your
television says to you: "Nicholas, while you were away I
looked at 350 hours of television this afternoon and I have
this great twenty minutes which I think you'll be interested
in seeing." That is indeed possible now by building
intelligence into a television receiver.

Nicholas Negroponte
Director
MIT Media Lab

Nicholas Negroponte is the soul of the MIT Media Lab. He
describes the vision, quoted above, as a world where human
beings are in complete control of the media surrounding them.
If the television signal comes in to your TV receiver in digital
form, there will be a computer built-in to your TV set. That
computer will have tremendous storage and processing power.
When you first buy it, you will answer a series of questions.
How old are you? Where did you grow up? What is your educational level? What are your hobbies? Where do your parents
live? The computer will then process and store your personal
profile. In a sense, your computer will know you.

As the digital signals bring in all your television services
throughout the day and night, the programs will be stored in the
computer's memory. When you come home and turn on the
television set a menu will appear. The first item on the menu
may be today's news program, but you will not have to wait
until 6 P.M., or 6:30 P.M. All you will do is push a button and
your news will begin. The computer will have monitored and
stored every news story, from every news program, that came
into your house that day. You will not have to watch a mass-
produced news program for an hour to see if there is any information that is of interest to you. You will simply be presented
a customized, personal news program that only contains the
information you told your computer you are interested in. For
example, if the computer knows that your parents live in South

Florida and there was a hurricane in South Florida today, that would be the lead story on your news program. For your next-door neighbor, who works for an airline company, the lead story might be about his company's announced merger with another carrier. As Nicholas Negroponte says: "Prime time is your time." Suppose it is 8:21 P.M. and you want to watch a movie. You will push a button and the menu will display the movies that your television set has received and stored since you last watched. Since the computer knows you like action-adventure movies, they will be highlighted for you. Next, you push a button to select the movie of your choice and up it comes. Gone is the fear that you missed something from yesterday. No longer do you have to wait until 10 P.M. to see a particular movie. Your movie begins at 8:21 P.M., when you want it. Prime time is your time.

Fiber-Optics

For this revolution that puts you in charge of scheduling your own custom-made programs, the phone company has to be authorized to deliver television programs to your house. The National Association of Broadcasters and the U.S. Telephone Association have started meeting to work out an agreement that will ensure that local broadcasting stations would be carried on fiber-optic lines. The cable industry is, of course, seriously concerned about the phone companies getting into the program delivery business, but the Bush administration, the National League of Cities, and the U.S. Conference of Mayors have all come out in favor of the telephone companies.

The phone company itself is taking the position that the whole world will be interconnected by fiber-optic wire. In fact, there is an enormous international effort, involving more than 100 countries including the United States, to link together all the phone systems in the world in a huge integrated services digital network (ISDN). The phone company says it stands ready to spend the estimated $450 billion required to upgrade the U.S. infrastructure if it is allowed to get into the television delivery business. Without being able to tap into a new source of revenue from television-related services, the phone companies argue that they cannot afford the expense, and they warn that if the United States doesn't upgrade its telecommunications infrastructure soon it will not be competitive in the global marketplace. To demonstrate how strategically important the television delivery business is, five of the seven telephone companies have invested hundreds of millions of dollars to build cable systems in the United Kingdom, France, and Israel. Most Washington experts take the position that it makes no more sense to delay the installation of fiber-optic wire than it does to stop paving roads. Although most expect plenty of political fighting before the issue is resolved, they generally agree that fiber-optic wires will be the transportation system that global telecommunications technology travels on in the 21st century.

As for Nicholas Negroponte's vision of the merging of televisions and computers: it has already begun. Radius, a California-based maker of high-resolution display systems and graphics generators, has announced the creation of the Radius TV system. They call it an integrated computer television, or ICTV. The system puts all the video and TV sources, like camcorders and video cassettes, broadcast stations and cable stations, under the control of a Macintosh computer. The viewer can freeze, store, and process the various sources coming into a TV in an infinite number of ways. The president of Radius has said: "This will result in an explosion of new applications that none of us can even imagine today."

Interactive TV

Implicit in the media lab's vision of the future is a revolution in the way that viewers will interact with their televisions.

> Now we are using computer intelligence not so much to filter
> programming but to compress it. You will be able to transmit
> one hour of video in five seconds. In that environment, your
> television set will pick off what you need. Stewart Brand,
> who wrote the book called *The Media Lab*, invented the term
> "broadcatching." It's the notion of allowing you to deal with
> several of what we call tell-me-mores. Dan Rather is telling

you what happened in Iraq today. If you are interested, you push the tell-me-more button and he elaborates. All of that is really possible, real soon.

Nicholas Negroponte
Director
MIT Media Lab

In Montreal, a cable company is experimenting with an add-on service called "videoway." About 30,000 cable subscribers pay around $22 per month for the videoway option. It allows viewers to watch the headlines on Metropole, a local Montreal station, and then choose which stories they desire to see covered in depth. Viewers also can watch a sporting event, and can see coverage of the event from two different camera angles by switching the videoway device.

I am a great proponent of interactive television. We, as a company, have spent a fair amount of time and energy following the development of interactive. First of all, if you look at the Nintendo craze, there are somewhere in the area of 23 or 25 million Nintendo gadgets sitting in people's homes. The Nintendo machine is a relatively sophisticated piece of equipment. A year ago, at Christmas time, there was marketed something called the Wheel of Fortune interactive television game. The television picture of Wheel of Fortune was actually encoded to interact with this black box that enabled the viewer at home to play against the studio audience on Wheel of Fortune. They sold a bunch of them. Unfortunately, it had only that one function. You could only play the Wheel of Fortune game with this relatively expensive piece of equipment. That was a very rudimentary form of interaction. But, I think it gave us a view of the future as to what might be possible in terms of encoding the TV picture to enable something to happen between the viewer and the screen as opposed to just sitting and absorbing whatever comes across.

We have been looking for the universal black box that would enable the viewer to do a number of things. For instance, product couponing. It's something that's doable today. It's just a matter of cost. Millions of dollars are spent each year by advertisers in newspapers to deliver coupons to the consumer's front door. The use of those coupons versus the distribution makes it one of the most expensive forms of advertising ever devised by man. There is a way electronically, through a thermal printer, to have a commercial appear on your TV set and within the commercial, if you are interested in a 75-cents-off offer that we will make for the next two products coming up, press your remote and the coupon will be printed right out of your set. So, all of those things are doable. One can call up if you're watching a sporting event and you're interested in some more information about a batter in baseball, and what his record has been against a pitcher; you can access in the corner of your screen, a whole range of data. That's doable today.

Herb Granath
President
CapCities/ABC Video
Enterprises

The FCC has approved an interactive broadcast service in Reston, Virginia. A company called TV Answer has developed an economical means of establishing a two-way TV service without requiring cable systems. The company says its system used set-top digital radio transmitters and satellites to link homes to a computer for processing orders. Mark Fowler, the former chairman of the FCC, represents TV Answer. He reportedly called the Virginia service a "step toward establishing a 21st century interactive TV system."

In terms of news and sports, I believe there is a possibility that this whole interactive idea may come into play. It is the situation whereby you have twelve different cameras shooting the baseball game and the guy in his seat at home can select whether he wants to sit on the first base line or whether he wants to become the catcher. He determines the kind of impact that he wants to have from that baseball game or football game at a particular point in time. Does he want to

concentrate on the quarterback? Does he want to see the
tackle block out the guard? What does he want to watch? I
think in terms of news and sports programming you're going
to see the opportunity to bring the viewer much closer into
the action.

> Ike Herbert
> Executive Vice President
> Coca-Cola Company

A rudimentary form of interactive television has already
proven its value. The use of 900-number phone responses has
grown from an estimated $500 million annual business in 1985
to a projected $2.5 billion annual business in 1992. The all-time
record for responses to a 900-number contest goes to Wheel of
Fortune. During November of 1990 the gameshow drew 4.7 million calls in three weeks in response to its sweepstakes program.
King World donated $1 million to the national Toys for Tots cam-
paign as a result of the revenue generated from the contest. Several program syndication companies have interactive or phone
programming divisions studying ways of applying advanced telephone technologies to television programming. And, the king of
gameshows, the inventor of Wheel of Fortune and Jeopardy,
Merv Griffin, is apparently developing the concept of interactivity. He has been quoted as saying that he thinks interactivity
could be an important element in the future of gameshows.

Interactivity between television viewers and their TV sets is
evolving at the same time as the development of what the computer industry calls multimedia. Multimedia is a generic term
that means the convergence of the technologies of video, audio,
laserdisks, and computer processors. John Scully, the chairman
of Apple Computers, has been quoted as saying, "Multimedia
will change the world in the 1990s as personal computers did in
the 1980s." Bill Gates, the visionary founder of Microsoft Corp.,
insists that: "Multimedia will be bigger than everything we do
today." The chairman of Sony, Akio Morita, addressed the Consumer Electronics show in Chicago in the summer of 1990 by calling for an industry-wide commitment to developing multimedia.
Morita said: "The creativity of technology leaders, combined
with the genius of software producers, will take us into this world

of interactive entertainment by blending the features of advanced video, audio, and computer technologies.''

There are many examples of the practical use of multimedia as an interactive communications tool in the worlds of business and education. Prospective Buick customers, using a floppy disk they receive in the mail or at the showroom, see animated pictures of the cars, with realistic engine sounds, on their computer screens. The multimedia shoppers can select various options for their dream car and watch the computer play out a program that calculates monthly payments and compares prices to Buick's competitors. Buick reportedly has sold about twice as many cars to potential customers who have interacted with the multimedia marketing program than they would to regular potential customers. The American Heart Association is reportedly sending interactive multimedia lessons to medical schools to teach students about managing blood cholesterol levels. Although multimedia is a computer technology and not literally a television technology, industry experts point to the development of multimedia as another example of how the world of telecommunications is coming together in a digital, interactive format.

High-Definition TV

The most heralded new technology in the United States is high-definition television (HD-TV). HD-TV promises to bring wide, crisp, movie-like pictures and compact disk-like digital sound to home TVs. Invented more than ten years ago in Japan, HD-TV has been controversial in the United States from the start. Some experts think it's much to do about nothing.

> Some people think the next revolutionary step in television is high-definition. That is a lot of rubbish. That is silly. If you walk down the street and ask somebody what's wrong with television, you're not going to find anybody who says: Resolution.
>
> Nicholas Negroponte
> Director
> MIT Media Lab

The government has spent years talking about HD-TV and trying to test various competing proposals so that an American standard can be established. The Advanced Television Test Center started testing HD-TV systems in April of 1991. The FCC is scheduled to select a standard in 1993. So, it will be at least the middle of the decade before HD-TV is seriously introduced in the United States.

I think high-definition television will find a very slow entry into the United States for a relatively practical reason. That is that the real value of hi-def TV really has to do with large screen resolution and most American homes are not of a dimension that will allow for huge television screens. On the smaller screen it is obviously an enhancement, but it's not so dramatic. It was at last year's cable show where a manufacturer made an enormous mistake. He announced that at his booth he would unveil before our amazed eyes this hi-def TV. They had three sets, side by side, one of which was our 525 system today. The second was what we currently call enhanced TV. We take our 525 picture and clean it up and present a much clearer picture. We can probably improve our current picture by somewhere near 40 percent without changing any technology. And, on the third set he had hi-def TV.

We all gathered out in front of his booth and at the proper moment the black covers were whipped off the sets and the same picture was on all three and there was this long silence as everyone looked at it. In the back of the crowd somebody said: Which one is the hi-def TV? It is that dramatic. It's not like the difference between a black-and-white picture and color. It will find its way into the new technology because virtually all the television sets are manufactured in Japan right now and they are pushing hi-def TV as a selling feature to try to sell a new generation of television sets. If you look at it from a consumer point of view, there are always those who jump on the bandwagon early so they can say that they are the first on their block to have it. But, for the average viewer to junk his current TV set and run out and buy an expensive new model, I don't think that's in the cards. However, as people wear out their televisions and have to replace them, they'll want to replace them with something that is state-of-the-art.

> Herb Granath
> President
> CapCities/ABC
> Video Enterprises

Six different systems are competing at the FCC to become the American standard for HD-TV. At the end of 1990, Zenith Electronics (the only American company still manufacturing television sets) and AT&T announced that they had developed a fully digital hi-def system. Zenith is the third of the six competitors to announce a digital system. A number of experts predict that one of the digital systems will become the American standard because approving a signal standard will speed up the generally anticipated marriage of personal home computers and television sets.

> The image of HD-TV in the early days was that it's like Christmas Eve and Santa Claus comes dropping down every single chimney in America and slips your old TV set into his bag and drops off the new one that has twice the clarity. Then you wake up and enjoy Christmas dinner and absolutely everything in your life remains the same except your TV set now has twice as many lines on it as it did before. That's the early vision of HD-TV. And that's the one that I think is worth trying to expand. Question one is that the industry has finally begun to understand and endorse and even adapt to increasingly sophisticated television systems in addition to ones that are just clearer. A lot of that sophistication is in services, but the level of sophistication associated with new TV systems is now fundamentally and vastly different than what the original approaches to HD-TV were. That's what I mean when I say that the battle has been won. We crossed the threshold where we are now thinking of TV as a digital processing system. We're not asking stupid questions like: Can we afford a frame-storer in every receiver? We're now talking about: What can you do with it? How can you use that to increase the sophistication of the

processing that goes on in the signal? That's the corner that
we have turned. We've made great strides in turning that
corner. That's the battle. And, the evidence is that of the six
credible proposals before the FCC almost all of them no
longer contemplate broadcasting pixels. They are
broadcasting highly processed transformations of the picture.
That's a significant thing.

Andrew Lippman
Associate Director
MIT Media Lab

Meanwhile, as the development of HD-TV marches on, station and network television executives worry about how they
are going to pay for the conversion from analog broadcasting
equipment to digital high-definition. Cameras, recorders, and
transmitters will all require upgrading.

The program production industry is gradually making the tran-
sition to hi-def facilities. There are now four such facilities in New
York and two in Los Angeles. NHK, the Japanese public network,
has opened a 10,000-square-foot HD-TV facility at the Kaufman
Astoria Studios in Queens. Rebo high definition studio produces
a hi-def music series in its facility. And, the Sullivan Theater,
which used to be a Broadway music hall, has been renovated into
a HD-TV post-production center. In Los Angeles, Sony has a
high-definition facility at the Columbia Studios lot. Rebo, the New
York hi-def outfit, has opened what it calls the first fully dedicated
HD-TV facility on the West Coast at the Hollywood Center lot.
All predictions are that the production community will expand its
work in the hi-def format throughout the decade.

Since HD-TV will probably take a good part of the decade
to become integrated into the television industry, a group of
broadcasters and cable TV networks have begun testing what
they describe as an interim solution to high-definition television.
The so-called Super NTSC system sharpens a small screen picture, but it does not involve a new TV signal. The backers of
the venture include CapCities/ABC, TCI Cable, Comsat Cable
Communications, General Instrument Corp., Scientific-
Atlanta, Viacom Cable, and Group W Broadcasting. The test
is designed to see whether viewers think the system is worth

paying for—and, if so, how much? The creator of the Super NTSC system says he wants his system to become the standard for improved television pictures until real HD-TV becomes widespread by the end of the decade.

Direct Broadcast Satellite

DBS, Direct Broadcast Satellite, is another new technology that has been trying to establish itself in the U.S. market for several years. At the beginning of the '90s its future remained unclear. Primestar, a DBS system owned by nine cable companies and GE Americom, the satellite company, is up and running. It offers seven superstations and three pay-per-view channels to customers who are not able to be served by traditional cable. In its initial launch phase, Primestar is being offered on a test basis in 38 American communities. The most sophisticated of the announced DBS ventures, Sky Cable, appears to have been dramatically trimmed back by its owners. Announced in the beginning of 1990 as a billion-dollar coventure between News Corp., NBC Cablevision, and Hughes Communications, it is unclear whether the service will actually get off the ground in the '90s. The third major DBS venture scheduled to launch is Skypix, which plans to offer sixty channels of pay-per-view movies and a package of superstations and cable networks. However, no official start date has been announced for the privately funded Skypix service. A number of analysts question whether DBS will grow into a major business in the United States during the '90s. They cite the fact that so much of the country is already wired for cable and that most viewers already have a wide variety of program choices. It's not a question of whether direct broadcast satellite services are an acceptable new technology. It's a question of whether there is a marketplace for the services.

Pay-per-View

Pay-per-view, commonly referred to as PPV, is the other new technology that is attracting attention at the start of the decade.

The industry reported that in 1990 the 32 pay-per-view events grossed $135 million, $120 million of which come from wrestling and boxing. Revenues from feature films accounted for an additional $130 million in 1990. Analysts will be watching several developments in the early 1990s before deciding whether PPV will become a major new technology by the end of the decade. First, NBC has announced that 600 hours of coverage of the 1992 Barcelona Olympics will be marketed as a pay-per-view event. Both the National Football League and the National Basketball Association have announced that they are considering experimenting with offering televised games on a pay-per-view basis. U.S.A., the cable network, is reportedly considering a package of regularly scheduled pay-per-view boxing programs. The performance of these PPV projects will significantly influence the future of pay-per-view in America.

> I'm not so sure that viewing is as aggressive as people think. I'm not so sure that the average viewer in the United States, given the opportunity to select a product on a pay-per-view basis, has the appetite to do that day in and day out. I think that as technology becomes more consumer friendly, and it becomes very easy to dial up a code and receive a program on a pay-per-view basis, there will be more of that. I think there is probably a need for both kinds of distribution: regular mainstream and pay-on-demand, which will certainly be stronger by the end of the decade.

> Kay Koplovitz
> President
> U.S.A. Cable Network

The Possibilities

The new technologies promise better quality pictures and computer-controlled television systems within the decade. Japanese manufacturers have been working for years to develop the new television screen that will display the more attractive video of tomorrow. The Sharpe Corporation has announced that it will have two full-color screens, one 9 inches and one 14 inches, on the market in Japan by the end of 1991. These so-called hang-on-the-wall screens will only be about an inch thick, and they will be expensive. The 9-inch screen reportedly will cost about $1800. The Sharpe liquid crystal display screens have what the company describes as a new active matrix system that controls each picture element thus ensuring bright, sharp reproduction.

I happen to believe that the TV set of the future will be something that comes down against your wall. It will be big screen projection. I think we're just liable to find people spending more time with it. I think what you will have in the year 2000, this is great to talk like this because I'll probably be retired by then and I won't have to worry about what I'm saying, you'll have a remote control in your hand and you will push one of three things. You'll push what I call a free button. There will be an array of forty or fifty channels that will have free television on it. It will be sort of a combination of what we now call the networks, independents, and basic cable. There will be another button you'll push and it will say subscription and those will be various services that you may subscribe to on a monthly or yearly basis. Maybe there will be an overall movie service, a Disney channel, a sports service, a news service. Those subscriptions will vary from seven or eight dollars a month to a dollar a month. But it will be something that you're paying for on a subscription basis. Then you'll push another button and it will be pay-per-view. That will be movies and events on demand. Your TV set will be built-in with multiple VCR recording capabilities. I think you're going to be able to say things to your TV like: I'm interested in buying a car. Record all the car commercials that come in for the next week and I'd like to look at them when I come home. And, it will stack them all up. And, the next time there's a Lucy show on, please record it for me. Here's what I'd like to see. I think all that is a real simple thing and it will just be built-in the machine. I think it will make using your television a lot more interesting. The picture will be better and the sound will be better. So, I think you may spend more time with it.

Rich Frank
President
Walt Disney Studios

The scientists and other professionals at the MIT Media Lab have projected the future of television beyond the year 2000. They have peered out over the farthest horizon of the known television universe. What they have seen there, a few more years into the 21st century, promises to make what we will experience in the '90s pale by comparison. Here is how they describe it in their fifth anniversary booklet:

> Our latest concept is variable resolution television, in which the aspect ratio, the number of frames-per-second, and the number of scan lines, can be adjusted to the requirements of the individual picture, TV receiver, or viewer's choice. Our longer-term view is that of model-based-video, wherein the camera, if it is called that, reports an accurate model in space and time, and the receiver generates the picture. In this manner you could view, for example, a baseball game from the perspective of the ball, something unrealizable with cameras, as such. In the much longer term, little holographic baseball players will run around your living room hitting and catching a 1/4 inch holographic ball.

The new technologies offer a fascinating vision for the future of television. It is a vision that is very different from the daily television viewing experiences of most Americans. It is a more active, involved experience. It is a much higher quality sensory experience, and it is much more viewer controllable than ever before.

CHAPTER NINETEEN

Television Citizenship

Throughout the media world in the programming business, in the advertising business, and in the news business, industry leaders predict that television will become even more important in our daily lives in the future. If that is indeed the case, it is appropriate to conclude the exploration of television's future by asking the question: If television is going to have a major social impact in the 21st century, what kind of citizen will it be? This is a question that will be answered, in large part, by the actions and decisions of the industry leaders whose corporate positions afford them a great deal of influence over the future of television. Their insights can reveal clues about the '90s. In the course of interviewing dozens of such people throughout the world, a clear pattern emerged. These are people who, in general, give a lot of thought to the issue of television's role in modern life.

Media Frontiers

Many industry leaders make reference to the historical social upheavals of the early part of the 1990s. They focus on the uncomfortable tension in a world where media frontiers are coming down much faster than political systems can adjust to the new social landscape.

I wrote a masters thesis twenty years ago: ''The Political Implications of Satellite Technology.'' What we see today, I think, in Eastern Europe particularly, and in the Soviet Union and the Baltic states, is clearly the result of communication that was no longer able to be thwarted. You really can't stop the communications of satellite technology the way you could jam the traditional terrestrial broadcasting. Once people have knowledge that they are so far behind Western Europe in development, there's only so much they can tolerate. Gorbachev is going to have a very difficult challenge. He can't stop what has started. The question is: Can those countries and regions generate the economic base that they need to really change? Because, it's not just the knowledge. It's really being able to develop the economic base that can turn around the economy of a country so it can operate on a free-market basis. If you go into the travel business, their insight will be that traveling has had a very big impact on people's ability to know and to change. So, each industry has some idea of how their industry has had an impact. I'm sure the computer industry has had a big impact because chip technology has really changed all these tools that we have. Look at the Chinese student revolt. I think that most of that information came from computer technology, and, to at least some degree from television reports. I think there are different industries that have had an impact. But, no question that the world is smaller. Every place is less remote.

Kay Koplovitz
President
U.S.A. Cable Network

There are thousands and thousands of satellite dishes in Eastern Europe today. But, long before the satellite dishes, there were VCRs. Videotapes of every description—movies, music videos, news programs, and documentaries—were smuggled into these countries and secretly distributed among the people. Despite the political and media frontiers in these countries, television has been the only real window to the outside world for many years.

It's my personal belief that television played an enormous role in bringing down the barriers between East and West in terms of political philosophy; the willingness of the Eastern Block people to continue to allow themselves to be dominated without having a voice in their own government. I believe that TV played an enormous role there. That, therefore, demonstrates to me the ability and power of TV to change people's attitudes and to change their actions. If that is so, it is incumbent upon us who are shapers of the content of television to be doubly sure that content reacts to positive results as opposed to the stereotypical attitudes of viewers. I think one of the great beneficiaries of that will be a much more thoughtful approach to the environment. I think we're seeing the beginnings of that right now. What other practical benefits will come of that, I leave to your imagination. But, I believe that the power of the medium has been demonstrated to effect change, and if you accept that, then the only question is what changes are we all going to experience. I think that it is probably bad news for those political systems that have traditionally relied on the lack of information and knowledge to the general public to exist.

Herb Granath
President
CapCities/ABC Video
Enterprises

China

China is, by far, the largest undeveloped television marketplace in the world. Even though Western programmers and advertisers occasionally fantasize about doing business in a place where there are a billion potential customers, they really don't have any illusions about China becoming a free-market democracy anytime soon. For a very long time, China has been in the serious business of preventing outside influences from permeating their society. But, even in China, where the government can prevent most citizens from knowing that a social revolution was attempted, television is credited or blamed—depending on whom you're talking to—for spreading the seeds of Western thought.

> I don't know whether things would have happened so fast. I can personally talk about China because I was personally very much involved there. I will tell you that before the Tienanmen Square situation I had two series on the air. One was Hunter and the other one was Falcon Crest. They were on the air twice a week; each one in four provinces. I got a 65 share of the audience, which translates into an audience of 450 million people. Tienanmen Square happened and Dan Rather was there. He came back from China and wrote an editorial in the *New York Times*. In that editorial he mentioned Hunter and Falcon Crest. Now, I'm not saying that Hunter and Falcon Crest were the dominant reason why the democratic movement took place, and why Tienanmen Square took place. But, it was influential. It's also interesting to note that not once during that whole situation did the government insist on taking those two programs off the air. And, the reason, I think, was that there were so many people watching it that it was a way to keep people home. So, yes, I believe that exposure to other people's ways of life certainly is very influential, especially in a third-world country where they can see Western-type programming. I'm not saying that Western-type programming is good or bad. I'm just saying that it's influential.
>
> Michael Solomon
> President
> Warner Bros. International

Europe

Because it is influential, Western programming remains controversial in many parts of the world. During the '80s in Europe,
for example, as new private television stations exposed people to
American programs for the first time, those American programs
were extremely popular. But, as the novelty wore off, ratings for
the American programs settled down and the locally produced
programs regained their popularity. When all is said and done,
people generally want to watch programs that reflect people
like themselves, but it is becoming more and more difficult to
legislate the flow of programs in a particular country. France, for
example, has established legal quotas designed to force increased
production of French programs and to limit the amount of imported Western programs during the '90s. The whole scheme
is threatened, however, by satellite broadcasting from other
Western European countries which do not fall under the jurisdic-
tion of the French laws. The issue of how to best stimulate local,
in-country production, will clearly be one of the most important
challenges facing legislators and industry leaders in the future.

> I think, in a kind of funny way, the Europeans are right in
> worrying about what the impact of expanded broadcasting will
> be on their cultures. It will, sort of, be a homogenization of the
> world. I see that as the cost. When you go all over the world
> and you see the same stores everywhere and the same goods for
> sale everywhere and McDonald's everywhere, places tend to
> lose something of their identity. And, I think that as television
> expands and becomes more homogeneous, it will have similar
> effects on cultural and social life. In a certain way it's healthy.
> Like most things in life, it's just a matter of balance. Whether
> it's what happened in Eastern Europe, or the fact that no
> matter how bad what might have happened in China was, if the
> world were not watching, it probably would have been a lot
> worse. We are a global village in a news and information sense
> today.
>
> Michael Garin
> Senior Managing Director
> Furman, Selz

Global TV News

The degree to which the world is a global village today has a lot to do with the vision of Ted Turner. The international television business has taken notice of the impact of CNN. Throughout the '80s, CNN's influence grew as it became a dependable source of constant information about whatever was happening throughout the world. By the early '90s, CNN's influence was so obvious and pervasive that one of the time honored rules of television, "Let no good idea go uncopied," was invoked.

The giant public broadcasting system in Japan is launching a global news operation, as is the BBC in England and a consortium of major public broadcasters in continental Europe. But, no one expects the upcoming competition in the global TV news business to dampen the zeal of the man who built CNN.

> The problems that the world faces now are global problems. Global warming is a global problem; the elephants, the whales, the rainforest, the quality of the atmosphere, the state of the oceans, overfishing, all require global solutions. There is a global network in CNN, and it is being watched by the leaders all over the world. The impact of it is great. How much of it is television and how much is just good common sense is just hard to tell. It's a combination of the two. But, right now all of the world leaders, when anything happens, can all tune to CNN and get the same information simultaneously. Democracy is definitely on the rise. People are going to demand a say in how they are governed. You see this in the major changes that have occurred in what was formerly called the Eastern Block.
>
> Ted Turner
> Chairman
> Turner Broadcasting System

TV 2000

A number of industry leaders predict that the quality and relevance of television's citizenship at the turn of the century will have something to do with its gradual emergence as a more intimate medium. This will happen, they project, when the technologies of television and computers are merged. Then, they say, the potential influence of television will really be felt.

> The power of communication; it just seems to me that it is impossible not to affect people by watching the massacre of black on black in South Africa, and the insanity of it all. As TV might become more interactive, people can begin to experience the dirt, the dust, the agony of war. It seems to me that they're going to want to avoid it a hell of a lot more than the sort of casual, intellectual approach to it that most people have today. I just think that ultimately that will be one of the positive byproducts of the future of television.
>
> Ike Herbert
> Executive Vice President
> Coca-Cola Company

There are high expectations for the value of television's citizenship in the next century. Those expectations are built on the belief that the pace of change during the '90s will be geometrically faster than during any previous decade and that the growth of television will be an essential element in the process. Not surprisingly, most industry leaders perceive television's role as a global citizen in positive, constructive terms. They predict that television will emerge from being a one-way source of mass market entertainment to being an interactive communications tool empowering viewers to enjoy and experience a dazzling new world of digital creations.

NATPE
INTERNATIONAL

NATPE International is the premier program industry
organization in the world. Based in Los Angeles, California,
NATPE International operates as a nonprofit corporation
actively serving the needs of a rapidly emerging global video
industry. Each January it stages the world's largest and most
important program marketplace, bringing together nearly
10,000 producers, distributors, buyers, financiers, advertising
executives, and press representatives.

Throughout the rest of the year, it provides a variety of
ongoing services to the industry and to its membership. The
NATPE International Education Foundation is one of the
most active components of the organization. Each year it
sponsors university faculty development programs,
educational and management seminars, and international
exchange programs. The Education Foundation is also the
producer of educational video programs and printed
materials, like this book, providing access to critical industry
information to NATPE members throughout the world.

For more information about NATPE International and its
member services, contact:

> Mr. Phil Corvo
> President
> NATPE International
> 10100 Santa Monica Blvd.
> Suite 300
> Los Angeles, California 90067
>
> Phone: (213) 282-8801
> Fax: (213) 282-0760

Index